Gateshead
Remembered

by Anthea Lang

I am Thinking of You at Gateshead

Home thoughts from abroad – a First World War postcard.

Previous page: A welcome party in Newton Street for returning Boer War soldiers.

Copyright Anthea Lang 2014

First published in 2014 by

Summerhill Books
PO Box 1210, Newcastle upon Tyne NE99 4AH

www.summerhillbooks.co.uk

email: summerhillbooks@yahoo.co.uk

ISBN: 978-1-906721-86-2

CONTENTS

A council dustcart transformed into Stephenson's 'Rocket' for the Gateshead Carnival, 1927.

Introduction

This book makes no claim whatsoever to be a definitive history of Gateshead. It is, however, a look at some of the main events and stories recorded in the newspapers of the day which have impacted on the lives of people who live here. From disasters and controversy, to restoration and regeneration, Gateshead people have seen it all. I hope I have shed new light on some topics and perhaps jogged some memories.

Acknowledgments

My grateful thanks go to George Nairn, Beamish Museum, the Progressive Players and Trevor Ermel for the use of some of the illustrations and staff at Gateshead Library, particularly Jenifer Bell and Maggie Thacker, for their help. Thanks are also due to Roger Fern for his advice and suggestions and of course to my publisher Andrew Clark without whose help and encouragement this book might never have seen the light of day.

Anthea Lang, November 2014

The Papermill Square Mission in the Teams area where the harmonium has actually been man-handled outside and possibly the whole congregation has gathered for the photographer. Note the two boys in the front row carefully cradling their pigeons.

Front cover
Residents of Bowl Alley Bank in 1929.

Back cover
Top: Miss Eva Johnson, Gateshead's Children's Librarian, helps a group of young girls with their homework in the Central Library in 1960.

Bottom: Residents of Allhusen Terrace pose for the photographer before leaving on their annual street outing in 1923.

Chapter One
Living in Gateshead

'There seemed a great deal of Gateshead and the whole town appeared to have been carefully planned by an enemy of the human race in its more exuberant aspects. Insects can do better than this: their habitations are equally monotonous but far more efficiently constructed.'

So said the author J.B. Priestley in his 'English Journey' written in 1934. Harsh words perhaps – however, throughout the book, he was arguing for social change. But when he came to Gateshead, things were already changing as a major slum clearance programme was taking place in the town, removing whole areas of sub-standard houses.

Turn the clock back almost 100 years, and December 1835 marked another turning point for some people in Gateshead. For the first time, they could have a vote for a candidate to represent them on the about to be formed Town Council. Until then, Gateshead had been governed by the Four and Twenty – a group of men based at St Mary's Church. These men were not elected, as membership usually passed down from father to son and had done so since the middle ages. Some had special responsibilities for law and order, others for maintaining roads but none could truly describe themselves as 'The people's choice'. That situation now changed although, for those living in the desperately overcrowded areas of the Quayside, Bottle Bank and the High Street, it would be some time before they would notice any discernible difference.

For these people, living in Gateshead wasn't a particularly pleasant experience. The number of immigrant workers who flooded into Gateshead from the 1820s onwards in search of work, resulted in more and more people living in a relatively small

Bankwell Stairs off Pipewellgate, around 1886.

area between the Quayside and the High Street. There is a record of one family of seven living in one room in Pipewellgate which they shared with a donkey! Whilst this is probably exceptional, census returns provide ample evidence of severe overcrowding and, until regulations were brought in, lodging houses could have as many as 40-50 occupants in houses designed for perhaps a quarter of that number. Beds were luxuries and even when available were often shared by four people – two by day and two by night. Toilets were largely non-existent, fresh water was a rare occurrence and many people were forced to live in conditions which could best be described as squalid. And even in the 20th century, a 1936 survey revealed Gateshead to be the second worst county borough in England with 15.8% of its population living in overcrowded conditions.

The worst areas in which to live were regarded as Pipewellgate, 'the island' – an area between Church Street and Bottle Bank – and the Irish stronghold of Leonard's Court off the High Street. Inhabitants in Leonard's Court had no access to either fresh water or basic sanitation and although conditions later improved, people were still living here in some discomfort until the 1930s when

Numbers 24-26 Leonard's Court just prior to demolition.

they were eventually demolished. Named after James Leonard, whose market gardens had once been here, this was the scene of 15 deaths in the 1853 cholera epidemic. In 1835, George Thew's lodging house was reported to contain *'two lodgers of very suspicious appearance and behaviour'* while the 1851 census revealed 342 people (64 families) living in 20 houses. Even as late as 1911, eight people could be found sharing one room. To celebrate the street's Irishness, a local wag wrote a poem about it:

> *Down in the district of Leonard's Court*
> *There lived a red-haired girl,*
> *One of a tribe called Mary McGee*
> *Face of a whisky shade.*
> *And every evening there came a Mick,*
> *Full of love and beer*
> *And in his pocket he carried a brick*
>
> *For if there's a rival near.*
> *Under the gas lamps light,*
> *He would yell with all his might –*
> *'Mary, Mary McGee,*
> *you are the girl I'm waiting to see,*
> *If you'll only marry me,*
> *I'll never work no more'*

There were some exceptions to bad housing and one of these was Hawks Cottages, built for his workforce by George Hawks who, in the 1840s, commissioned the successful architects John & Benjamin Green to design and build accommodation for his workers on land close to his iron works. The Gateshead Observer of 3rd March 1849 proudly announced the establishment of an embryo town – 'New Gateshead'. Had it been successful, this would have been part of the contemporary movement for building 'model' industrial settlements, like others at Saltaire and New Lanark. Sadly, financial constraints seem to have prevented the dream of this new town becoming a reality and only Hawks

Cottages, two rows of ten houses built opposite each other joined at one end by a more substantial house (for the foreman of the works), were built. Each terraced cottage contained four rooms including a closet, boiler, oven and sink – far in excess of what many working people were used to at the time and which could easily have been described as 'model homes for workmen' (*right*). When these cottages were demolished in the 1960s, it was a source of some regret to many of their occupiers.

Another serious attempt to build better worker's housing was made in 1837 with the development of an area in the town centre which became known as 'Barns Close'. Designed to attract regular wage earners, these were substantial terraced houses with cellars but built with a fatal flaw – no drainage. This meant that within a few years, they became riddled with damp resulting in their occupants living in sub-standard conditions.

The houses were demolished in the 1950s and not before time. They were the subject of a housing inquiry in 1932 after the roof of one house fell in leaving 54 people homeless.

Of course, for those who could afford to, there were alternative areas of town in which to live. Within central Gateshead, both Walker Terrace and Regent Terrace were designed for the middle classes and if a degree of travel was acceptable, there were always the new suburbs of Bensham and Low Fell both created by enclosure awards in the early 19th century.

Left: The rear of Brunswick Terrace and Melbourne Street in the 1930s.

Bensham – Gateshead's first suburb

When an area of the town fields was enclosed in 1814 and divided up among the borough holders (descendants of people who had held certain medieval properties to which borough rights were attached), the scene was set for a whole new area to be created. Bensham was ideally situated – its high position above the town meant it was clear of the noxious smells of the industrial quayside and provided an oasis of calm for its inhabitants. So healthy was it that in the 16th and 17th centuries plague victims were moved here and housed in little wooden huts which would be dismantled once the outbreak had passed, then re-erected when another outbreak occurred.

Elizabeth Spence Watson in the dining room at Bensham Grove.

The iron founder William Hymers started the building process by building a terrace of 10 fine houses (more houses were added later) called Claremont Avenue in 1819. Others, including Sedgewick Place, Woodbine Terrace and Barrington Place soon followed and until the 1860s Bensham was regarded as a very middle class area. Some substantial houses were built here including Bensham Tower, Barrington House, Bensham Grove and Woodbine Cottage. Today, Blue Heritage Plaques remind us of some of the people who lived here – the Liberal politician Robert Spence Watson, GP Dr Alfred Cox (later secretary of the British Medical Association), William and Catherine Booth (who would go on to found the Salvation Army) and Emily Davies, educationalist and Suffragist.

Further land was sold to Richard Coxon Young, a builder and joiner in 1849, for £1,400. Substantial looking terraces were built here which included Hutt Street, Hall Terrace (both now demolished), Union Row (later part of Coatsworth Road) and Collingwood Terrace (later part of Bensham Road). These were all substantial terraces as can be seen in the following photographs.

Ravensworth Terrace, another in the series was dismantled and rebuilt at Beamish Museum where it can still be seen today. It wasn't long before the area was populated with public houses and shops.

A rather sad picture of Hall Terrace during demolition, 1971.

Alice, Jane and Daniel Ord outside number 8 Hall Terrace, 1900.

Bensham Avenue with its corner shop and gas lamp.

From the 1870s however, the character of Bensham began to change as speculative builders bought up vacant areas of land and built a whole series of streets, largely containing Tyneside flats. Now, the working classes flocked to Bensham and the area began to lose much of its middle class appearance. Woodbine Street was built in 1891 on the site of the old Union workhouse (which had lent its name to Union Row), virtually the instant it was demolished. The backs of Sedgewick Place were extended with shop fronts on Coatsworth Road while the gardens of Woodbine Cottage were removed and Villa Place built in their place. During the 20th century, many of the large houses began to disappear but enough of the early terraces remained to give Bensham a character all of its own. It also became home to Gateshead's Orthodox Jewish Community.

Hutt Street, 1970.

Right: The 19th and 20th century versions of economy of space – Overhill Terrace and Bensham Court in 1977. (Photograph by Trevor Ermel.)

The seriously better off in Gateshead had the wherewithal to buy large estates on which they would typically build a large mansion, a lodge or two and stables. Take a trip along Durham Road in Low Fell today and you can still see the evidence of this.

Gradually as the 19th century wore on, estate owners realised the potential of selling some of their land to speculative builders. One of the most successful of these was William Affleck who is credited with the concept of designing the first Tyneside flat – the Victorian answer to economy of space and overcrowding. These flats were built in ever increasing numbers throughout Gateshead and whole areas of the town including Saltwell, Bensham and Shipcote soon became full of them.

Heathfield House on Durham Road, built for Joseph Willis Swinburne in 1856.

Another developer of the Tyneside flat was John Ross who bought the four acre Bensham Hall Estate from the Crawshay family and built more new flats in Stirling Terrace, Dunsmuir Grove and Kelvin Grove. An upstairs flat in Stirling Terrace could be rented for 7/- a week whilst the downstairs flat, with one room less, cost 6/-. These were superior Tyneside flats with a working scullery and a kitchen reserved for dining. Rents in other streets were 5/4d for upstairs and 5/- for downstairs.

In 1888, the 28 acre Rodsley Estate (named after Rodsley House which formerly occupied the site) was sold for 7/6d a square yard and the Avenues were built, most being designed by Lawrence Armour, a Scottish civil engineer and town councillor.

But there was still a problem as large numbers of sub-standard housing remained, despite legislation from 1875 onwards which gave councils the power to demolish slum dwellings. House building stalled during the First World War but as men returned home there was a national demand for 'homes fit for heroes' and a new type of housing developed – the Council house. Sixty-five acres of land were bought with a recreation ground (Hodkin Park) at Sheriff Hill and the foundation stone for the new estate was laid by Ald. Clough in October 1920. Even though a shortage of bricks caused building delays, by 1922, 232 houses had been built with rents set at between 10/6d and 15/- per week depending on the number of rooms. By 1930, another estate at Carr Hill estate had been completed, Sheriff Hill had been expanded and tennis courts had been provided.

In the older houses however, sanitation remained a problem with nearly 75% of houses in 1920 having no flush toilet. Thanks largely to the efforts of one man, Councillor and Chair of the Public Health Committee, Peter Strong Hancock, who encouraged the council to apply for a government grant, 18,706 houses were converted from earth to water closets between 1925-27. The time originally estimated had been nearly four times this period. Due to his efforts (and his initials) Hancock was thereafter given the nickname of 'Pully String' Hancock!

Road laying at Sheriff Hill.

Under the Housing Act of 1930, the Council were given much greater legal powers to deal with the problem of slum housing and in 1933 another act, forcing councils to make slum clearance their main priority, finally meant the demise of the old slums on the Quayside and the town centre. Pipewellgate, Hillgate, Bridge Street and Church Street together with many of the old courts all disappeared from the Gateshead landscape. With a five year plan, nearly 1,000 families were moved to Council houses.

Hillgate being demolished around 1930.

A view of the Chandless area looking down Burdon Street just before demolition

The housing which replaced them photographed in 1962.

1937 proved to be a peak year for house building with 887 new homes. Of these, 424 were council houses (this compares with 50 built in the first year in 1921). Unfortunately once again, war halted building plans. However, the 1950s saw a resurgence in house building but this time in another new form– the high rise block.

The first high rise flats on Tyneside opened on the former slum clearance area of Barns Close in July 1955. Each had gas heating and cooking with a drying cupboard, refuse disposal, chutes and a lift. Other high rise blocks soon followed at Priory Court and Regent Street and a new slum clearance development at Chandless replaced what had sometimes been referred to as a Dickensian 'rookery' – an area of hundreds of tightly packed poor quality Victorian terraced housing.

Gateshead's progress in slum clearance was huge – between 1945 to 1961 more than 1,600 slum dwellings were cleared and more than 6,000 people were rehoused.

However, high rise blocks proved not to be the whole answer to slum clearance and caused problems all of their own. In an effort to combat this a new 'village' scheme was designed and Clasper Village and St Cuthbert's Village were born.

St Cuthbert's Village was built by Stanley Miller and was the biggest single housing project ever undertaken in Gateshead (Stanley Miller also constructed multi-storey blocks at Beacon Lough, Allerdene and Harlow Green).

St Cuthbert's Village was described as 'a brilliantly clever housing scheme' when it was formally opened by the Prime Minister, Harold Wilson in April 1970. The village contained 15 tower blocks of varying heights all of which had deck access. However, anti-social behaviour led to it eventually being demolished and Clasper Village is now also under threat of demolition.

New materials were introduced after the war to provide a quick and cheap solution to post war housing needs. Dorran houses, delivered in three sections, which could be built in 24 hours and ready for occupation in three weeks were built at Wrekenton and Saltwell, while Orlit flats (made of pre-cast reinforced concrete) were built in 1953 on Saltwell Road.

Victorian 'posh' houses in Regent Terrace contrast with the working class 20th century high rise Regent's Court.

Dorran houses in Ventnor Crescent, Saltwell.

Warenford Walk, St Cuthbert's Village, 1986.

Low Fell had seen an upsurge in house building in the 1930s in the Valley Drive area and there was a further resurgence after the war, with new council estates at Cedars Green, Harlow Green and Allerdene and residential estates such as those in the Chowdene area. Low Fell already had its own Victorian 'garden village' at the north on the Musgrave estate but a further garden village was built by E.P. Calderwood in 1931 for Durham County Council – the estate was then outside the Gateshead boundary. Roads were tree lined and all the houses were built with gardens. They were also wired for

Palmerston Walk, Clasper Village, around 1970.

wireless reception with aerial and roof wires contained within metal tubes run under the plaster. Calling a street after its builder was not unusual. It merely carried on a longstanding tradition with older streets such as Affleck Street, Brewis Street and Cowper Street all named after their builders.

Many of Gateshead's old streets are now no more. Often they were demolished because of their low standard but others fell victim to developers or, as The Crescent did (*right*), to new road systems.

Of course, not everyone living in Gateshead had their own house, flat or tenement and for those who couldn't support themselves, there remained only one option – the workhouse.

Gateshead had first illegally appropriated Thomas Powell's 17th century alms houses on the High Street which they used in the early 19th century as a poorhouse but in 1841 a new workhouse was constructed in Bensham on what is now Woodbine Street. Men, women and children were all segregated and families were kept apart. Despite this however, three female inmates were discovered to be pregnant by other inmates and severe overcrowding meant children were often sleeping three to a bed. To improve matters, land at High Teams was bought and a new workhouse opened in 1890.

Gateshead was fortunate with this workhouse – the matron was well regarded and food was usually of better quality than might perhaps have been expected. Each Christmas, members of the great and the good of Gateshead would descend on the workhouse and ceremoniously carve the festive roast. For Christmas presents, the men usually got beer, together with pipes and tobacco while the women got tea. *(Below: Despite the pictures on the wall, the women's ward, photographed in 1906, still presents a fairly dismal picture.)*

Later the workhouse was renamed High Teams Institution and following the creation of the National Health Service in 1948, Fountain View was created from the non-hospital wards and housed 302 men and women designated as 'aged and cripples'. By now, there was at least a degree of entertainment – in 1950, a weekly cinema was operating here as well as dances, concerts and bus trips.

Things did move on for the elderly and infirm in Gateshead and in 1950, the foundation stone for Beacon View at Beacon Lough was laid. This could house eight men and eight women each with their own bedroom and male and female sitting rooms. Eventually, there was one of these homes on each Council estate in Gateshead although all have now closed as privately operated facilities have expanded.

A 'Meals on wheels' service had begun after the Second World War – elderly Gateshead residents could pay 1/- for a tinned meal. (*The photo left shows a delivery to two elderly residents in the 1970s.*)

Facilities for children began to be seen as more important in the 20th century. Cottage homes at Shotley Bridge had been built early in the 20th century for Gateshead's orphans and abandoned children but by 1960, two children's homes were operating in Gateshead – Briermede and Oakfield – while Earlswood nursery catered for the under fives.

Although Gateshead was by no means a centre of crime, living here wasn't always particularly safe and, not surprisingly, given the number of public houses in the town, drunkenness was a constant problem. One of the biggest lists for drunkenness ever heard at Gateshead was that following the peace celebrations at the end of the Boer War. The local cells could not hold the number arrested and many had to be sent to Durham. However, it has to be said that some of the worst culprits were the police themselves. In 1844, after Gateshead police had gone to Newcastle to help with a bunch of rowdy soldiers, it was claimed that the Gateshead men had given them intoxicating liquor while transporting them to the cells. It was therefore *'resolved that the practice of giving prisoners intoxicants should be discontinued.'* And very often, members of the force would be caught drinking after hours in public houses – after, of course, they had cautioned the landlord that 'last orders' had to be called!

Not surprisingly, given the squalid conditions, one of the worst areas for crime was Pipewellgate (*below*). In 1890, the body of a clerk at Taylor's Boiler Cement Works was

found lying on the ground outside an office. Another serious crime was that of the murder of Mary Ann Smith of 22 Pipewellgate, whose bruised and bloodstained body was discovered in the family's water closet on 27th December 1897. Her husband Charles was accused of the crime and, despite his pleas and a petition of innocence, he was hanged at Durham on 22nd March 1898.

The police cells in Gateshead were only used to hold men and women prior to sentencing. When the new Town Hall was opened in 1870 there was a glowing recommendation for its police cells which were described as *'perfectly lighted and ventilated. The warming can be regulated to any temperature, and being cleanly whitened out, they present as comfortable an appearance as it is desirable that such places should.'* They would certainly have been an improvement on a previous 'lock-up' on Bridge Street which was in such bad condition a prisoner once escaped simply by knocking a wall down!

Gateshead's police force had its origins in the watch men of the Four and Twenty but once the town had its own Council, six constables were appointed – but only to work on Saturdays and Sundays. Gradually, the force was expanded and the first detectives were appointed in 1861.

Crime wasn't always easy to detect on the often dark streets of Gateshead. In 1825 only six streets were lit. Originally, whale oil was used but later, gas was supplied. It was not until 1948 that Gateshead began to change its gas lamps for electric lights and the lamplighter with his ladder became a less frequent sight.

The Police Band in 1876. The bandmaster, John Amers is on the left of the front row.

Gas was supplied by the Newcastle & Gateshead Gas Company who had built new premises at Redheugh in 1876. It was a ready source of energy and was gradually found in most homes in Gateshead. The Gas Company held a competition for their workers in 1905 to design an advert to encourage more people to use gas. (*The advert is below.*) Ironically, although Joseph Swan, inventor of the incandescent electric light bulb had lived at Underhill at Low Fell (the first house in the world to be lit by electric light), many people in Gateshead were still relying on gas light until the late 1950s.

Until the advent of the motorised fire engine, a fire was always a particular hazard. From 1857, a volunteer fire service began, using members of the police force armed with wooden rattles to raise an alarm. In 1862 a manual fire engine, police axes, buckets and eight leather helmets were bought and in 1871, a wooden fire escape was added – a wheeled ladder with an extension to help firemen reach upper windows. At first, they had to draw their water from plugs and stand pipes but in 1892, the fire brigade became a separate institution of the police service and in the same year, a new steam fire engine which could discharge 350 gallons of water per minute was bought at a cost of £540. A fire alarm bell was also fixed in the clock tower above the police station. However, as the men first had to return to the Town Hall to change their uniform and harness the horse and fire engine, their response to an emergency was not necessarily particularly quick!

In 1904, a new house was bought in Swinburne Place for the chief fireman and in 1907 a fire station and gymnasium was built. During the Second World War, a sports pavilion on the Team Valley Trading Estate was used as a temporary fire station but this closed when a new station opened in 1964 on the site of Dryden's farm at Shipcote. This was recently replaced by another fire station.

The firemen outside Swinburne Place in 1907. Note the rather fetching 'French berets' of the firemen – unfortunately of little safety benefit.

Of course, a ready water supply was essential and in the early days, this was a real problem. Many of Gateshead's old wells had become blocked through industrial waste and standpipes weren't always where they were needed. In 1845, only 110 out of 3,495 houses had a water supply but once the Newcastle & Gateshead Water Company took over the supply in 1854, things slowly began to improve.

Communications also improved as the years went on. A rather sporadic postal service had begun in the 1830s but improved through the 19th century with up to four deliveries of mail per day. Gateshead's first telephone kiosk appeared in 1924 outside the Town Hall and within a year, six more had appeared. Ten years later, radio reception became easier when the Rediffusion service began. Gateshead became the main control point for Rediffusion's distribution system in County Durham and by 1950 they were supplying radio broadcast programmes to three out of every five homes in the town. Television soon followed and in 1953 when Pontop Pike was due to begin transmission, Gateshead residents were confidently promised improved reception in time for the Coronation.

This chapter began with one of J.B. Priestley's scathing comments about the Gateshead he found in 1934. He continued to condemn the town by saying *'The town was built to work in and to sleep in. You can still sleep in it I suppose.'* Well, had he visited Gateshead in the 1960s, he would have seen a town in which the central area was being virtually completely rebuilt. Gateshead residents must have felt they were living in a permanent building site with new houses, new road systems and new shopping centres taking place around them. As will be seen in other chapters, 'Gatesiders' have lived through periods of industrial expansion, depression and more recently regeneration. Gateshead was, and still is, a changing town.

Chapter Two
The Best Days of Our Lives

Children at Kells Lane Board School, 1900.

Introduction

Before the mid 19th century, many children had no 'best days of their lives'. Childhood was something simply to survive and by the time a child was 12, he or she might have been working for four years or possibly even more. What education poorer children, in particular, received might be haphazard (or non-existent). From the 1840s onwards however, things began to change as various reforms began to happen, and less was left to chance.

One of these reforms was Forster's Education Act in 1870. For the first time, towns and villages had to have enough school places for their children to be educated. Those schools already in existence had to reach a certain standard – if they didn't, they would not be counted. A census of the number of school aged children (between 5-13) in each town was taken and then compared with the number of satisfactory school places available. If there was a shortfall, then towns could create their own School Board. It was the responsibility of the School Board to ensure that there were enough school places available in their area and they could obtain government grants to enable them to do so.

When the results of the census in Gateshead was compared with the number of school places available, there was a shortfall of over 5,000. Gateshead's School Board was the fourth in England and Wales to be created and the committee was elected by the voters. It included the Rector, at first Edward Prest (succeeded by William Moore Ede), Elizabeth Spence Watson of Bensham Grove and many of the town's industrialists. As well as building new schools, the School Board could take over existing schools, so long as they reached a certain standard.

Types of Schools

In 1874, Gateshead's first new purpose-built Board School opened at Prior Street, and Alexandra Road Board School followed the following year. Within the next 30 years, 21 new schools had opened in Gateshead and in the four years between 1874 and 1879, 5,794 school places had been established. In 1880, education for children up to the age of 11 was made compulsory, although it wasn't free until 1891 (the School Board was allowed to pay the fees of the very poor). They were also allowed to purchase existing

The school shown in this 1928 photograph is unnamed but it could have been any one of a number of Gateshead Board Schools.

schools which were not already being run by the Board, as they did with the Boys' High School on Prince Consort Road. However, this wasn't popular with all schools. The Lady Vernon National School on Derwentwater Road stated that *'Should anything precipitate the declining of the Vernon Day Schools, the premises MUST ON NO ACCOUNT be given up to the School Board or anybody.'*

The design of Board Schools tended to follow a standard pattern. They usually had separate boys and girls entrances and a common feature (such as at Kells Lane Board School) was a central hall on each floor with classrooms surrounding it. Schools outside the auspices of School Boards included many of the Church Schools and the National Schools, although many of the latter either closed due to lack of funds or became Board Schools within a few years.

While the Board schools initially concentrated on what we would regard today as mainstream primary education, they gradually added other types of educational buildings such as the Higher Grade Schools and the Industrial Schools. In 1891, a new Higher Grade School opened in Whitehall Road (this had been operating in temporary premises since 1884) and in 1894, the former Boys' High School was purchased and became an additional Higher Grade School (this later became the Grammar School). The photograph right, taken in 1889, shows girls from the Higher Grade School with the headmaster (later Professor) Mark R. Wright at the left. Even when free education was available, this didn't always cover fees for those children who wanted to go to these schools and so scholarships were often keenly tried for.

This photograph shows the boys at Kelvin Grove Board School who were scholarship winners in 1912. All the boys are very smartly dressed with a few of them wearing bow ties.

One of the less successful schools operated by the School Board was the Day Industrial School on Windmill Hills. Gateshead already had an Industrial School (the privately endowed Abbot Memorial School (*see page 20*) but this catered largely for child criminals). The Day Industrial School, would, it was hoped, deal with problem children. This is a photograph of the building which opened in October 1880 – the small building to the left was an infants' school. However, it transpired that not only were the children 'difficult', but so too were the parents, who very often neglected their parental duty to send the children to school. Truancy was high, with many parents refusing to pay fines for non-attendance. The children themselves were described as '*wretchedly clad, filthy in person; they are not in a fit state*

for association with other children.' The school closed in 1895, by which time only 43 children were still on the register.

By the 1890s, a school building programme was well under way and Brighton Avenue Board School was only one of a number which opened in this decade. Among its first intake were children from Bensham workhouse who had previously been educated at a small school actually within the workhouse itself. In 1901, they left the Board School as they were moved out of the workhouse to new 'cottage homes' near Shotley Bridge.

The School Boards were abolished in 1902 and their duties were transferred to Local Education Authorities (LEAs). But Gateshead's School Board had already done sterling work in terms of education provision in the town and laid the foundation on which future education in Gateshead would be built. As the 20th century progressed, more and more schools would be built in the town. Some were built to serve new estates and others to replace older buildings. As the school leaving-age was raised, new secondary schools were needed. Following the 1944 Education Act, which created grammar schools, the Secondary School was renamed Gateshead Grammar School. This was later demolished and replaced by Saltwell Senior High. In 1956, a new Girls' Grammar School opened on Dryden Road and an additional Grammar School, Heathfield, opened a few years later on Durham Road.

There were other schools, however, than the Board/LEA schools.

Private Education

Notable local Quaker families, including the Spence Watsons, encouraged the Girls' Public Day School Company (later changed to 'Trust') to open a new high school in Gateshead in 1876. This was established first in a private house (Prospect Cottage at Bensham) but soon moved to new premises at Windmill Hills. Over 300 girls came here from a wide area. The school closed in 1907 (the building was later the Labour Exchange), and merged with their previous 'feeder' school in Eskdale Terrace, Newcastle to become the Central Newcastle High School for Girls.

The Gateshead High School for Boys opened in 1883 on Prince Consort Road but had a short life, closing after only 10 years. Both these schools suffered from the popularity of the School Board's Higher Grade School on Whitehall Road.

Another girls' private school was established at R.S. Newall's former home, Ferndene, in 1906 and this was the forerunner of La Sagesse Convent School in Newcastle upon Tyne. The photo right shows some of the girls at Ferndene in 1911, the year before it closed and staff and pupils moved to their recently purchased Jesmond Towers.

In the 1920s, three different private schools opened in Gateshead. What was described as a 'Private School for Young Ladies' opened in Ravensworth Castle in 1921. Unfortunately, this wasn't very successful and lasted less than 10 years. The other two schools had longer lives however. In 1928, Beaconsfield School, owned by George and Lina Biltcliffe, began in Joseph Swan's former house, Underhill, at Low Fell and ran very successfully until closing in 1976. Musgrave Preparatory School on Durham Road, opened a few years before Beaconsfield, continued until 1999.

Left: The junior classroom in Ravensworth Castle, 1921.

The Abbot Memorial School

The Abbot Memorial School was founded by the widow of John George Abbot – the son of John Abbot, who had founded what became known as the Park ironworks (*see page 32*). Catherine was well known for her charity having also funded the old Northern Counties Orphanage on the Great North Road. She gave £9,473 which was £2,000 more than the building cost and laid the foundation stone on 17th October 1867. The school opened as an industrial school in January 1869 for 100 boys and 50 girls although, from 1907, it was boys only. These were children who had either already committed crimes or were thought to be potential criminals. The girls were trained for domestic service whilst the boys learnt a trade. However, the school was criticised in its later years, as many of the boys simply ended up in the pits. The school was very successful, particularly in its early years. Between 1882 and 1884, out of 87 boys and girls discharged, 75 were described as '*doing well*', four had died, five were unknown and only three were leading what were termed '*doubtful lives*'. The boys had their own gardens and sometimes went to summer camp – in 1921 they were taken to Warkworth.

The school closed on 31st March 1930 when the remaining boys were transferred to Axwell Park at Blaydon. However, a trust fund supported many boys and girls after the school was closed – in 1940, 98 boys and girls were given grants for a variety of purposes including clothing, bicycles for travel to work and apprenticeships. One was even given money for driving lessons. The catchment area for the school comprised the whole of the North of England.

The boys' daily timetable in 1917

6.00	Inmates rise and make beds
6.30	Prepare rooms for industrial employment
7.30	Ablutions and recreation
8.00	Breakfast (bread, dripping and cocoa)
8.30	Recreation
9.00	Inspection: Scripture lesson, hymn and prayers
9.30	Schoolroom or workshop
12.30	Prepare for dinner
12.40	Dinner (stew or hotpot)
1.00	Recreation
1.45	Ablutions
2.00	Schoolroom or workshop
5.00	Ablutions
5.20	Tea
5.45	Recreation
6.00	Recreation in summer; evening classes in winter
7.30	Supper for Juniors; Juniors retire to bed (bread &cheese)
7.45	Supper and prayers; Seniors retire to bed (later in summer).

Joicey Road Open Air School

The idea of open air schools for delicate or consumptive children came from the continent and spread to England during the early 20th century. The benefits of children being educated in a healthy atmosphere away from crowded conditions were obvious. When this school opened in 1937, it was seen as something of a pioneer in the area as it was designed to educate children of all ages and cared for 'physically handicapped and delicate' children from Gateshead. The school medical officer selected the children – they included not just disabled children but also those suffering from TB, respiratory diseases and polio. One feature of the school was that each afternoon, the children were expected to have an outdoor nap unless it was raining in which case all the windows and doors were opened. The photograph right shows the children taking an indoor nap in 1949.

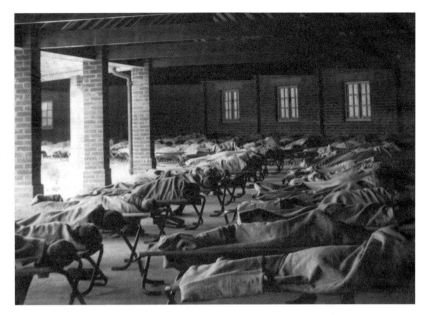

Nursery Education

The very first nursery school on Tyneside was established in Gateshead in 1929. It opened in the hall at Bensham Settlement (formerly Bensham Grove). However, these premises weren't ideal as they had to be shared with other groups, which meant all equipment had to be constantly moved and re-moved.

Lady Astor contributed £1,200 which provided the basis of a building fund. The new nursery was formally opened in the grounds of the Settlement by Lady Astor's son, the Hon. William Astor in 1931. It was a spacious and airy building with large windows and a verandah.

The nursery catered for the children of the poor, the unemployed or those whose parents were ill. Many of the children came from severely overcrowded homes (even in the 1930s there were instances of a family of nine and another of seven, each living in just one room) and priority was given firstly to the health of the child and then to the home conditions. The nursery could take 55 under fives (later extended to 100) but there were always more children than places. No fees were charged other than 2/- each week for food. But even that was out of the reach of many families and so schools in the area began to 'adopt' a baby at the nursery. This happened to little three year old Jean Ellis, one of a family of six with a father in ill health and unable to work, who was 'adopted' by girls of Heaton Secondary School in Newcastle who each gave 3d – enough to keep Jean at nursery for one year.

The new nursery building in 1936.

Some very prominent visitors came to the nursery as can be seen in the photograph right. Edward, Prince of Wales, was presented with a tea pot lid by a little three year old and it was noticed that he was particularly interested in those children who wore leg-irons. These were often used to correct bone deformities due to rickets – a disease often seen in malnourished children (which many of the children were when they first attended the nursery). The secretary of the Settlement later wrote to the Evening Chronicle praising the children, '*The children at the Bensham Grove Nursery School did not crowd around the Prince nor cling to him. Nursery school children have better manners.*'

Five years later, his brother George, the Duke of Kent, also visited the nursery and in the same year, the broadcaster and author Stuart Mais visited and later wrote '*By far the best sight at Bensham was that of 55 small infants wrapped in red blankets having their midday sleep in the nursery school.*'

However, not everyone agreed with the idea of a nursery, including a number of Gateshead Councillors who felt that a nursery was a wrong use of resources and mothers should be expected to look after their children in their own homes. But there was a real need for a nursery in

The visit of the Prince of Wales on 26th April 1932.

Gateshead. Families were large and very often in poor health and some mothers, living in unsanitary overcrowded conditions, simply couldn't cope. Bensham nursery was the first, but other nurseries were to follow in Gateshead.

So, these were some of the types of schools operating in Gateshead. But when you got to school, what did you do when you were there?

Lessons and Learning

To begin with, learning was very much taught by rote with monitors taught by teachers, and the monitors themselves, then teaching others. It was repetitive and often taught solely to the requirements of the various 'standards'. Classes were not organised by ages but by abilities and usually if a child reached a certain standard and had reached a minimum age, they were allowed to leave school earlier than the compulsory leaving age. Unfortunately, a number of schools in the poorer areas of Gateshead were criticised for having too many older children in lower standard classes.

Education revolved around the basic core skills – reading, writing and arithmetic (the three 'R's). Religious teaching was offered but in non-Church schools (i.e. the Board Schools), had to be non-denominational and was not compulsory. The School Inspector became a familiar sight – but not always a welcome one, as the amount of money schools received, was in direct proportion to the success of the School Inspector's visit.

Early lessons tended to be fairly static, with children sitting in rows of small wooden desks as can be seen in this photograph of Sunderland Road Infants taken in 1913.

Gradually, physical exercise began to be incorporated into schools, with yard drill a common sight. This photograph shows a girls' gym lesson in the Central School, Whitehall Road in the 1920s.

Sometimes lessons were taken outdoors as in this photograph above, taken in 1928, of an outdoor geography lesson at the Central School, Whitehall Road.

At the Secondary School, doing homework was seen as an essential part of day to day school life. In the 1940s, younger pupils were expected to do one and a half hours homework each evening and more as they grew older. Parents were warned that *'neglect of home lessons invariably results in unsatisfactory progress.'*

As time went on, the variety of lessons increased. The following two photographs show a boys' woodwork lesson and a girls' domestic science lesson at Gateshead Grammar School in 1949.

O Mother!

JACK THOMPSON HAS SUCH A NICE PAIR OF CORD KNICKERS FOR SCHOOL WEAR.

HE GOT THEM AT

SYKES' 284 High St., Gateshead.

AND SUCH A LOT TO CHOOSE FROM. DO GO AND SEE THEM.

What you wore at school, of course, (unless uniform was required) was usually what could be afforded. But just how many mothers bought these cord knickers for their boys as a result of the advert left which appeared in 1905?

Sports, Games and Events

Sport became seen as an essential outdoor activity, with football being very popular with boys. Kelvin Grove School had a very successful football team. Here they are in 1921 with their blackboard proudly proclaiming *'Winners of Bagnall & Watson cups. Runners up in Western Divn of Ncle & District Schools League.'*

Above: And here are the Kelvin Grove School football team again – this time the 1947-48 season.

Right: Sunderland Road School's football team at the end of the 1924-25 season.

*Above: The Boys'
Grammar School football
team in 1968.*

*Left: The Secondary
School girls' tennis team
in 1918.*

*Below: Members of the
tennis team at the same
school (but now known
as the Grammar School)
in 1947.*

Yard games were popular too as shown in the photograph above. The game played here is described as 'captain ball' which was a variant of basketball.

School days could be broken up by the arrival of the 'nit nurse' and by attendances at the school clinic (*see page 67*). But there was also patriotic Empire Day to look forward to. This involved the children dressing up in a variety of national costumes and learning and demonstrating new skills such as highland dancing. These celebrations were often attended by the Mayor. In 1931, the then Mayor, William Hall, said '*I ask you to realise that you belong to the greatest Empire the world has ever known ... so live clean, upright, noble lives.*'

Following the activities in the morning, children were then given the afternoon off school.

Empire Day at Sunderland Road School in 1929.

Right: This photograph shows the Mayor, William Pickering, and his wife, at the celebrations at King Edward Street School in 1939.

There were also educational visits to venues such as the Shipley Gallery. This photo shows the Gallery Curator, Matthew Young, talking to a group of very attentive boys from Gateshead Secondary School. The boys certainly didn't have far to travel as both buildings were next door to each other.

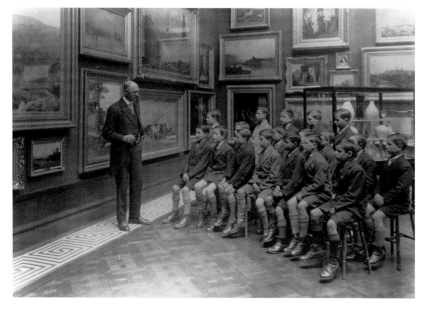

Many children were involved in the Pageant of Youth in 1927 which was a four day fête for charity held in Saltwell Park. It was organised by Gateshead head teachers and included various displays and tableaux from each school. Alexandra Road Boys' School performed 'Robin Hood' while 'The Pied Piper' was performed by Brighton Avenue Boys' School. The fete began with a mannequin

parade by the Co-op, sheepdog trials, side shows and stalls and there was singing on the lake by 'Miss Prior and her Blackbirds'.

In 1953 all schools were caught up in festivities to celebrate the Coronation of Elizabeth II. In this photograph, children at Prior Street School are about to practise their maypole dance before performing it in Saltwell park as part of the Coronation celebrations.

Right: Children and their teacher looking at the Shipley Gallery's Coronation exhibition which includes the crown jewels. Sadly, these were only replicas and not the real thing!

School Dinners

Gateshead was a pioneer in the world of school dinners and cheap school dinners in particular. When the Rector, William Moore Ede, discovered that many children were simply falling asleep at their lessons due to malnourishment, he realised something needed to be done. He decided to copy a scheme he had seen in Sweden which produced mass meals for school children. Going one step further, he even invented a special oven in which to cook the meals. This 'penny dinner' scheme operated for many years in Gateshead from 1884. For 1d a day children could have soup, pease pudding and either rhubarb or raisin pudding. Free school meals for the poor were introduced by the Liberal government in 1906 and in 1944 free school meals were introduced for all pupils. However, in 1949, a flat fee of 6d per meal was introduced – a fee which gradually rose as the years went on.

School dinners were not always universally liked but judging by the faces of the girls at Gateshead Grammar School shown below in 1949, they weren't too unhappy with what was on offer.

Holiday Camps

Many of the poorer children got the opportunity to go away to annual holiday camps. The first appears to have been at Blackhall Rocks, near Hartlepool and in 1933 there was an appeal by the Mayor, Timothy Armstrong, for money to support this initiative as ' … *the camp is doing a most beneficent work amongst the most needy of our children.*' The camp catered for 320 boys and girls giving them the ' … *health giving benefits of sunshine and sea air.*'

Right: Getting washed at Blackhall Rocks holiday camp, c. 1935.

After the Second World War, Dukeshouse Wood was used and provided 120 Gateshead children over 12 years old with a two week holiday. Activities included cinema shows, outings and socials as well as games. The children slept in dormitories in huts, all of which were named after trees.

The two photographs below perhaps demonstrate what the children who appear on them might very well have thought of as 'the best day of their life' at that particular moment. The first shows what was described as 'a poor bairns outing' from Burns Street in 1904. The children certainly are from poor backgrounds – only one child (possibly the photographer's son) is wearing shoes.

Left: This photo shows some children from Bensham Settlement Nursery waiting for the 'Silver Jubilee' train (high speed for the time) to pass in 1936. The photo was probably taken at Bensham station.

Chapter Three
Going To Work

A visitor to Gateshead in 1780 would have found most people doing similar jobs to those they would have done in medieval times. Farming or milling were typical of the kind of work carried out and so was coal mining although this was in decline as most of the pits were waterlogged and largely unworkable. Gateshead looked over enviously to its more profitable neighbour Newcastle.

One of the last mills standing in Gateshead was this one at Bensham.

However, return in 1880 and a visitor would have found a very different Gateshead – a Gateshead whose economy depended largely on heavy industries and whose population now contained a hefty proportion of Scottish and Irish immigrants or their descendants. A whole range of new and strange accents could be heard in Gateshead's workforce. And come back another hundred years later and the Gateshead worker would, again, have very different employment. The industrial expansion of the 19th century did not continue in the 20th, with the depression hitting Tyneside hard. Some of the old trades lingered on into the 1930s – a 1935 trade directory still shows a bonesetter, charcoal manufacturers, clay-pipe makers, cork cutters, lamp-black manufacturers and tallow brokers working in the town. But these did not survive the Second World War. However, once the new Team Valley Trading Estate opened in 1937 (*see page 38*), a whole range of new job opportunities came to Gateshead.

But to understand these changes, we need to take a closer look at those industries which did so much to contribute to the employment and ultimately the unemployment of so many Gateshead people. Workers' employment began to change in Gateshead from the early 1800s onwards with the appearance of gas works in Pipewellgate in 1819, a date which is widely regarded as the beginning of serious industrialization in the town. Pipewellgate and Teams to the west and Hillgate and Saltmeadows to the east of Gateshead were the main areas where the 19th century job seeker could find work as these areas had easy access to the river to transport goods and, unlike the rest of the town, were flat.

Typical of the early industries here were the limekilns, boat builders, glass works, rope works and small iron works. As the century progressed, the glass, rope, iron and gas works all developed and expanded, and further industries such as chemical works and railway engineering began. As word got around that work was becoming widely available in Gateshead, the town became popular with the hordes of Irish and Scottish labourers who travelled the country seeking employment. This suited the employers. They could pay cheap wages and largely disregard safe working conditions, as any man who complained could simply be dismissed, the employers confident in the knowledge that another 10 might be waiting to take his place. However, this was not true of all and certainly, it would appear that the iron firm of Hawks Crawshay did take some steps to ensure that their workforce had better working and living conditions than many. They built workers cottages (*see page 6*) and had their own school for their employees' children. Even so, until the Factory Acts of the 1840s which established working hours for children, Hawks' young employees were expected to work a 12 hour day in summer and an 11 hour day in winter.

George Hawks, Mayor of Gateshead and head of the firm.

By 1839, about 800 men and boys were employed by Hawks, with wages ranging from 22/- per week for a skilled tradesmen to the typical labourer who could only expect to take home 2/- per week – unless of course, he had drunk most of it in one of the numerous public houses. Hawks continued to expand throughout the 19th century but finally paid the price of over-enthusiastic expansion and closed in 1889, proudly proclaiming that all their debts had been paid.

A similar firm was that of John Abbot founded in 1770. From small works at Bush Yard, Oakwellgate, employing about 30 men engaged in making brass, copper and pewter, John Abbot expanded, leasing extra fields to the east of Oakwellgate and the firm became known as the Park Works. By 1889, these works covered 14.5 acres and employed

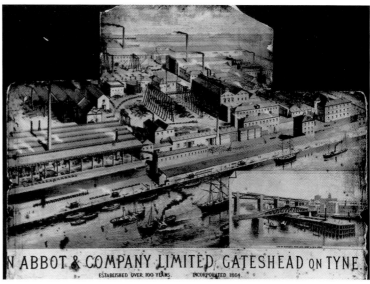

Part of an advert for the Park Works.

between 1,500-2,000 men. Abbot's were particularly well known as hydraulic engineers but they increasingly began to produce a wide range of items such as locomotive engines, capstans, water pipes, safety lamps – even tin tacks.

Eventually, this complete lack of specialization led to trouble and, like Hawks had done 20 years earlier, the firm went into voluntary liquidation in October 1909.

One 19th century firm which has continued into the 21st century is that of Clarke Chapman's (now owned by Langley Holdings) which began in 1864 as Benning, Clarke & Co, at the Victoria Engine Works, South Shore. They were one of the few firms to last through the depressions of the 1880s and 1930s. They took new premises at St James Road in 1874 (by which time they were Clarke, Watson & Gurney) and began making winches, but were soon producing boilers and electricity generating plants for ships. During the 20th century, they were also involved with nuclear engineering. In 1882, Charles Parsons joined the firm and carried out early turbine experiments at Park House (once the home of Gateshead's 'Lord of the Manor', William Cotesworth) which had become the drawing office for Clarke Chapman's. In 1887, Park House also became the home of the Sunbeam Lamp Company (formed by Clarke Chapman's two main partners, William Clarke and Abel Chapman, together with Parsons) which claimed to be the only factory outside London producing Swan's electric incandescent light bulb.

A group of Clarke Chapman's employees in 1915.

Other industries which often concentrated on the quayside area included glass making, rope making and cement production. The glass making industry never employed the thousands that Hawks and Abbot's did but still provided substantial employment – not just for those directly involved in producing it, but also the hawkers who slept in the factories during the night so they could collect their glass wares first thing in the morning. The two main firms in Gateshead were Sowerby's and Davidson's. Sowerby's established their Ellison works in East Street around the mid 1850s. They had begun earlier in the century producing flint glass but their fortunes were transformed when they began producing pressed glass (the poor man's cut glass) from the 1850s onwards. In 1889, the firm formed a subsidiary 'fine art' firm – the Gateshead Stained Glass company – in which the principal employees were also shareholders. In the 1920s, Sowerby's began producing cheap, but decorative, iridescent glass known as 'Carnival' glass. The firm was taken over by Suntex Safety Glass in 1957 and closed in 1972.

Sowerby, Gateshead

Trademarks of Sowerby's and Davidson's glass.

Davidson's glass works in the Teams area were Sowerby's main competitors. They were established in 1868 and, like Sowerby's, also produced pressed glass. Throughout the 19th and 20th centuries they concentrated on tableware and produced many varied colours, styles and patterns. One of these was Pearline wares – glass which was clear at the base and opaque at the top. This proved popular and was frequently copied by other manufacturers. Like Sowerby's, Davidson's were eventually taken over and in 1968 the works became known as the Brama Teams Glassworks. However, the

George Davidson, Gateshead

fuel crisis of the 1970s affected their furnaces and the firm eventually closed in 1987 after 120 years of glass production in Gateshead.

The 19th century saw the rise of Trade Unions to protect the interests of their employees. In the North East, the main glass workers union was that of the Pressed Glass Makers Friendly Society – a union which George Davidson seems to have cordially disliked – frequently ignoring their guidelines. The main bone of contention was payment. Employees in the glass works received a fixed amount of money for every 100 pieces of glass they produced. However, any glass damaged in the furnace (over which the workers had no control) was not counted and this always caused friction between management and workers. Under union rules, men started work at 5 or 6 am on Monday and worked eight hour shifts ending no later than 6 am on Saturday morning. Union members paid 1/- per week in return for which they received sickness benefits.

Another place of employment was the rope works which were situated in the Teams, South Shore and Hillgate areas. Rope works had existed in Gateshead from the 17th century but by far the best known firm was that of Haggie's who were awarded a prize at the 1851 Great Exhibition. Their female workers became known as Haggie's Angels due to their rather unangelic language! The firm made hemp and wire rope and had rope works at the South Shore and Hillgate. In 1845, the firm produced a rope measuring three miles long, eight inches in circumference and weighing 13 tons for the Liverpool and

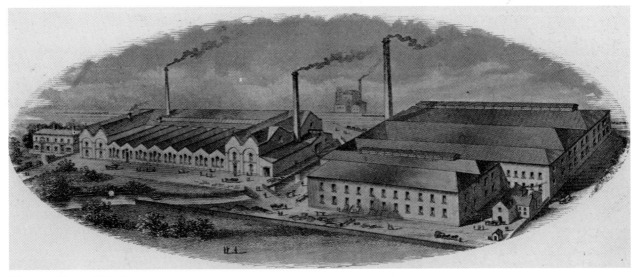

Teams Rope Works.

Manchester Railway. It was too heavy to be moved by horses so had to be taken by barge to Redheugh where there was access to the railway. Throughout the 19th century, Haggie's continued to expand and by 1907, 5,000 tons of wire rope were being produced. The output increased during the First World War and in 1926 the firm joined the British Ropes combine.

Other rope manufacturers were Robert Stirling Newall and Dixon Corbitt whose works were based in the Teams area. Like Haggie's, they also produced wire rope but R.S. Newall claimed the credit as the first person to patent the idea of housing a telegraph cable within a wire rope. In 1850 a cable was laid underseas for the first time. Although it only lasted a day, Newall had proved that the idea worked. The following year, Newall discovered that a competitor, Edward Weatherley, was producing an armoured cable for underseas use and sued for infringement of his patent. Newall's subsequently constructed a successful cross-Channel cable which brought many new orders for cable to the firm and now began to work in partnership with Corbitt's (the two firms later amalgamated) who produced the fibre cores for Newall's wire ropes.

Eventually Hood Haggie's took over both firms and were themselves subsequently taken over by Bridon Ropes.

But it was Greenesfield engineering works which became Gateshead's largest employer. In 1852, the North Eastern Railway (originally the York, Newcastle & Berwick Railway) opened their locomotive works at Greene's Field when they converted the former Greenesfield station buildings. Two years later, Greenesfield became the main locomotive works of

Staff at Greenesfield engineering works.

the newly formed North Eastern Railway (NER) and by 1855 were employing 200 engineers. At first, the work concentrated on engine repair but within a few years large scale locomotive building had begun. By 1883-4, the works had considerably expanded; by 1896, they were the town's largest employer and by 1909, over 3,300 men were employed at Greenesfield.

Next to the works was a large engine shed with five turntables, which was capable of housing 76 locomotives. However, the firm realised further expansion on the site was impossible and so the locomotive building part went to Darlington. Locomotive repairing

The remains of the pumping engine at Friar's Goose.

continued at Gateshead until 1932 when, despite a Council petition, the LNER decided to close the works. Although they re-opened in the Second World War, they finally closed in 1959.

The railways had developed as a result of the coal industry. Coal had been a lucrative product in medieval times but as the surface coal was exhausted, pits had to be dug deeper. Water ingress became a real problem, the industry declined and it was not until the development of improved steam pumping engines in the 19th century that there was a revival. The main pumping engine for this area was built at Friar's Goose. In 1844, this was stated to be the most powerful on the Tyne – it was about 180 hp and was capable of drawing off one and a half million gallons of water per day. The main collieries to be worked in the 19th century included Gateshead Park Colliery, Oakwellgate Colliery and Redheugh. Redheugh was the last to close in 1927. It reached its peak towards the end of the 19th century when it was employing about 420 men and boys and producing 120,000 tons of coal a year.

Gas and tar were by products of coal. Following the first gas works in Pipewellgate, new gas works for the Newcastle & Gateshead Gas Company were opened on a 25-acre site at Redheugh in 1876 which cost £100,000. Town gas was manufactured by heating coal in the absence of air in specially built retort houses. The retort house, shown below during demolition in 1981, was opened in 1896 at a cost of £1,000.

Miners at Redheugh Colliery about 1920.

The gas holders, which can still be seen today, were erected in the 1890s and continued to produce gas until the switch to North Sea Gas in the 1960s. During the Second World War, women were employed at the gas works as can be seen in the photograph below.

Redheugh gas works during the Second World War. At the front is Mrs Armstrong and behind her is Mrs Isabella McMillan.

The chemical works in 1907.

Bleach packers at Allhusen's chemical works.

If you were prepared to risk your health for a good wage then you might have been attracted to the chemical industry which had developed in the Saltmeadows area of Gateshead. The photo right shows some of the highest paid employees – the bleach packers – with their rather primitive pieces of flannel used to prevent inhaling poisonous fumes.

Allhusens was the best known chemical firm, and employees here were generally well looked after by their paternalistic employers who provided both schools and recreational facilities for them, and this generated loyalty to the company with generations of the same family working for the firm. The work was hot and thirsty and it was not uncommon for workers returning after the night shift to knock up a publican at 6.30 in the morning. A heavy sleeper would often be rudely awakened by stones or even half bricks being thrown at his pub door which were referred to locally as 'Irish confetti'!

However, by the early 20th century the chemical industry was in decline and, as new processes were devised which depended less on the large quantities of coal previously needed, production moved from Tyneside to Teesside. By the 1930s the tall chimneys shown in the photograph top left had been demolished but the resultant spoil heap which remained took years to clear.

Considering Gateshead's river frontage, you might expect many people to have been employed in shipbuilding. Despite author Daniel Defoe's comment in 1710 that '*They*

build ships here to perfection – I mean as to strength and firmness and to bear the sea', by the turn of the 19th century the trade was declining and by the 1830s, there was only one shipbuilder and two boat builders working in Hillgate. The main shipbuilding was now further east at Tyne Main where Gaddy & Lamb established a patent slipway in 1847 and at Friar's Goose where T. Mitchinson Ltd were still using a slipway until the mid 1960s (*right*). Boat and shipbuilding had

led to other associated trades such as block and mast makers, rope and cord makers and chandlers but these too were declining from their earlier numbers.

Gateshead Council however had big plans for the riverside and a Corporation Quay was mooted which would have involved the destruction of Hillgate. In the event, the Great Fire of 1854 did the destruction without any other help. It was hoped to obtain revenue from the North Eastern Railway which would potentially have been its chief customer, but negotiations proved unsatisfactory.

The quay was finally built in 1859, but on a much smaller scale, and was always underused in contrast to Newcastle Quay, just across the river, which was frequently congested. To increase business, two new sheds and a canteen were built by Wright Anderson & Co of Gateshead in 1922. The first steamer to arrive was the SS Arkleside of Ghent which unloaded a cargo of 7,830 barrels of apples and pears. The quay was eventually regarded as a white elephant, and in 1929 and 1930 disaster struck, when large sections of it fell into the Tyne. Repaired, it continued to provide employment for some years but not always for the industry for which it was intended – in the 1980s, the Quay became the mooring place for the Tuxedo Royal and the Tuxedo Princess floating nightclubs!

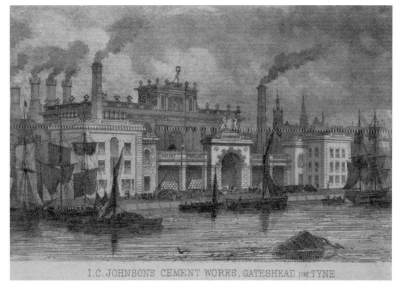

I.C. JOHNSONS CEMENT WORKS, GATESHEAD on TYNE.

The grand Italianate frontage of the image shown right belies the fact that this building was, in fact, the cement works belonging to Isaac Johnson. Isaac Johnson was quite a character. He lived until he was 100 and was still riding his penny farthing bicycle until well into his nineties!

Johnson's cement works became the first outside London to manufacture Portland cement from chalk, which came in as ballast in returning collier ships. However, by the late 1860s, ships had switched to water ballast, and so the supply of chalk ballast dried up. Johnson now had to bring up fresh chalk from Kent where he had another plant. During the First World War, the plant lost its chalk supply and this, coupled with a rapid rise in the price of raw materials, led to the work's eventual closure in 1924.

Shops provided a steady form of employment, particularly the larger shops such as Shephard's or Snowball's. Snowball's (*see also page 54*) treated their staff well, giving them half day holidays and arranging sports days for them. Shephard's too, were also regarded as good employers.

Shop workers usually survived the various trade depressions but for those employed in factories, foundries or gas works, it was a different story. The First World War meant a momentary boom in employment, but unemployment began to rear its head immediately afterwards. The many women who had worked so hard doing men's jobs during the war now had to return to life as housewives with any job opportunities reserved for the returning men. However, there now weren't enough jobs to go around and poverty started to rise in Gateshead. By the 1920s, Gateshead, in common with the rest of Tyneside, was classed as a derelict area. The majority of the industries which had been so successful 50 years earlier had disappeared – Hawks' and Abbot's iron works, Greenesfield Railway works, the chemical industry and many more. Glass making and rope production continued but the industries which had once employed thousands were no more.

Even some of the smaller industries, such as the clay pipe makers, found themselves redundant. Clay pipe production had been a feature of Gateshead from the 17th century and by the 19th century, this had become a popular home industry. New pipes were always needed as they were relatively fragile and frequently broke. In the early 19th century there were at

Joe Hardy, Gateshead's last clay pipe producer, at his work on Bankwell Stairs. He produced his last pipe in 1935.

least 10 pipe makers and even by the end of the 19th century, six were still in business using white china clay imported from Devon. However, the rise of the cheap cigarette meant the demise of the clay pipe, and soon, no one was making clay pipes in Gateshead any more.

For those without employment opportunities, the future now seemed bleak. In 1934, there was even a newspaper appeal for local employers to take on one man for one day in the run up to Christmas.

The slum clearances of the 1930s provided some work for the casual labourer but as can be seen in the photograph on page 10, this often involved a fair degree of danger. Other employment opportunities were created specifically for unemployed labour. This included street surfacing and road laying – something which seems quite a puzzle to these gentlemen! (*right*)

Another scheme operated at Saltwell Park where unemployed men were employed for shifts of three days per week in building a rose garden in 1935. Schemes like this weren't new however. In 1890, unemployed men had worked on levelling the site for the new workhouse at Bensham in exchange for being given poor relief.

In September 1931, an unemployed men's club was established at Bensham Settlement. The men built a hut in the grounds where they made articles for their homes, and in the run up to Christmas, children's toys. They weren't allowed to sell these goods however as their unemployment benefit would have been stopped. They also studied a wide range of subjects in the hope, often forlorn, that this would provide them with better employment opportunities.

Jobs were, quite literally, fought over. When the then new Jackson's model tailoring factory on Gateshead High Street advertised for its first intake of staff in 1931, a crowd of about 500, mostly boys and girls, rushed the entrance and swarmed over the building, completely out of control. The police had to be sent for and one local newspaper reported the manager as saying *'Girls and men fought like cats in the corridor and it is really a miracle no one was hurt.'*

However, new opportunities were just around the corner. The Team Valley Trading Estate was about to be built.

Team Valley Trading Estate

The North Eastern Development Board was formed in 1935 as a direct result of the depression years. In the October, they issued a report recommending the establishment of trading estates. Various sites were visited by Malcolm Stewart, the Government Commissioner for the Special Areas, and in May 1936, the North Eastern Trading Estates

Limited was formed. Initially, the favoured site was the Saltmeadows area of Gateshead but, almost at the last minute, the site location was switched to the Team Valley.

Construction began in August 1936 with George Wimpey & Co being given the contract for the construction of roads and services. The 700-acre site of the Team Valley was well situated for light industry although much work had to be done to it.

Traditionally pasture land, the site was boggy and subject to frequent flooding as can be seen in this photograph of the river Team in flood in 1886 at the south end of the valley (*left*).

Before construction work could begin, the area had to be stabilised with millions of tons of colliery waste. The river Team (locally known as 'the gut') which ran through the site had to be canalised and cleansed

The main road through the estate, Kingsway, was 174 feet wide, which made it, at the time, the widest road in Britain, and was constructed 'of the latest non-skid materials'. Crossing it was a slightly smaller road which ran from Low Fell station to the old Coach Road and where the two roads met was where the estate office was sited. Factories were situated 30 feet from the road and each had its own drive and car park. Side entrances were staggered so that main traffic was never directly crossed. A promotional brochure confidently expressed the hope that *'In the placid valley of the Team is being created a centre of light industry destined to set a lead for the whole country to follow.'*

The standard size of a factory was anticipated to be 6,000 square feet which could easily be increased to 8,000 and 12,000 square feet if necessary. As well as factories, which could be built and ready to move into within 75 days, there were other buildings on the estate including two garages, two banks, and a post office. The first firm to move onto the estate was Havmor Ltd (meat pies and sausages) and other early firms included Cadbury's, Sigmund Pumps, Hunter's the bakers (who supplied Sunblest bread and also supplied bread to Carrick's shops), Mellolite Ltd (lampshades) and Hugh Wood & Company (later Huwood) who made mining machinery.

Kingsway under construction in 1938.

The estate became the world's first Government sponsored Trading Estate and was formally opened on 22nd February 1939 by George VI (*right*).

In 1950, flour milling, once such a feature of medieval Gateshead, returned to the town with the opening of the Baltic Flour Mill, owned by Joseph Rank. It was situated by the river, because its grain supplies came in by sea, and could be unloaded straight into the mill. Like so many other planned developments in Gateshead, this had to be put on hold because of the outbreak of war in 1939. Designed by Gelder & Kitchin of Hull, the mill cost £1,500,000 and covered 81,000 square feet and could produce 240 tonnes of grain per hour. In 1957, the mill was

extended to include an animal feed mill. The Baltic mill eventually closed in November 1982, and most of it was demolished, finally ending Gateshead's milling tradition for good. The former grain silo has survived as a reminder – after a long time abandoned, it was converted to the Baltic Centre for Contemporary Art which opened in 2002 – a rather surprising but effective use of the previously derelict building.

Left: Baltic Flour Mill.

Chapter Four
Getting Around in Gateshead

Mail and passenger coaches were once frequent sights on Gateshead roads with regular services to Edinburgh, York and London but Gateshead was also one of the earliest railway towns, and when the Metro electric railway system arrived in 1981, many people did not realise this was just the latest chapter in the town's long history of railway development.

As early as 1838, the Newcastle and Carlisle Railway was running trains from a little temporary station at Redheugh (just below where the King Edward VII bridge is today) and the Brandling Junction Railway started a passenger service the following year which ran to Monkwearmouth and South Shields. This operated from a highly raised station platform at Oakwellgate – necessary to avoid trains crossing the High Street. Few people today parking their cars at Sage Gateshead's elevated car park realise this was once a busy railway station. Busy, but not lucrative, as the Brandling Junction Railway Company soon ran into financial difficulties and the service ended in 1845.

By now, however, the horizons and ambitions of the railway companies and their promoters had widened, with plans for lines to London and other places. And so another bigger and better station was built further west at Greenesfield. This tall single storeyed building faced north over the town with a spacious booking hall and represented the latest in station design with separate waiting rooms for first and second class passengers. Third class however had no such luxury! The station was built to a design of George Townsend Andrews of York and built by Charles John Pearson, a leading Gateshead builder and former Mayor of Gateshead.

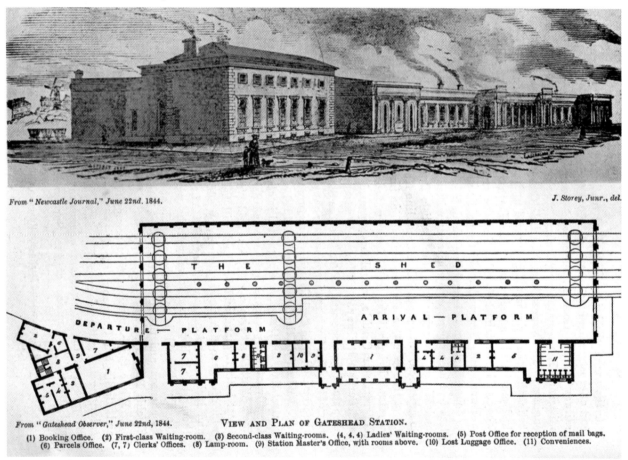

From "Newcastle Journal," June 22nd. 1844.   J. Storey, Junr., del.

From "Gateshead Observer," June 22nd, 1844.   VIEW AND PLAN OF GATESHEAD STATION.
(1) Booking Office. (2) First-class Waiting-room. (3) Second-class Waiting-rooms. (4, 4, 4) Ladies' Waiting-rooms. (5) Post Office for reception of mail bags. (6) Parcels Office. (7, 7) Clerks' Offices. (8) Lamp-room. (9) Station Master's Office, with rooms above. (10) Lost Luggage Office. (11) Conveniences.

View and plan of Greenesfield Station.

Celebrations took place when the first through train from Euston, London arrived on 18th June 1844 – the day the new line was formally opened. Travelling at an average speed of 37mph, the train had left Euston at 5.44 am and arrived in Gateshead at 2.24 pm. The scene now seemed to be set for 'Glorious Gateshead' and a station hotel was built to house passengers, who if they wished to continue their journey north, either had to walk across the Georgian Tyne Bridge or cross the river by boat. Greenesfield was now seen as an area of future development and the Council decided to move their civic headquarters here from Oakwellgate. However, the railway company's main objective in the area was Newcastle, across the river, and then the link onwards to Scotland. So, Greenesfield's days as the Tyneside terminal for London trains were numbered. Hawks Crawshay, who had supplied the ironwork for the station, now had a hand in its eventual demise when they won the contract to supply most of the iron work for the new High Level Bridge – a bridge over which trains could steam onwards to Newcastle and Scotland. Formally opened by Queen Victoria and Prince Albert in 1849, George Hawks proudly led Gateshead's civic procession wearing his newly purchased set of mayoral robes. As he ceremoniously hammered in the last rivet on the bridge, he hammered Gateshead's Greenesfield station into oblivion.

West Street Station with a 'Roedeer' engine steaming in.

However, while the passenger station might have gone, the station building was converted and developed instead for locomotive building and repair. In 1854 it became the main locomotive works of the newly formed North Eastern Railway (NER) and by 1901, the works were the largest single employer in Gateshead with more than 3,300 workers. However, lack of space eventually proved an issue and locomotive manufacture was moved to Darlington in 1910 with Greenesfield being used as a repair facility until closed by the LNER in 1932. A civic deputation failed to save it and nearly 1,000 men became unemployed as a result. The works re-opened during the Second World War but eventually closed in 1959.

The town's railway network meanwhile had expanded. The new Team Valley extension line (which resulted indirectly in the demolition of the Town Hall at Greenesfield) opened in 1868 with Gateshead West Station designed by Thomas Prosser built to serve it. Seventeen years later, another new station appeared in Gateshead when Gateshead East Station opened in 1885. This became the town's main station and stayed open until the new Metro system began.

Gateshead East Station, 1952.

The 20th century saw the eventual closure of all the Gateshead stations. The little Redheugh terminus closed in 1903, Low Fell closed in 1951, Bensham in 1954 and Gateshead West in 1965.

Right: Metro passengers alight at Gateshead Interchange.

The hilliness of Gateshead always presented a transport problem. Before the new Durham Road was opened in 1826, all north-south traffic had to use the steep incline of Sheriff Hill. Whilst the Durham Road considerably eased this problem, the use of horse-drawn trams (as introduced into Newcastle in 1878) was not really an option for Gateshead. So, steam traction was chosen when trams were introduced in Gateshead. The start of Gateshead's trams came in 1879, when a group of local business men formed themselves into a company to make and maintain a system of tramways within the town.

The Gateshead and District Tramways Act 1880 was given Royal Assent on 12th August 1880 but never implemented and a second amended act was passed in 1882.

The first two tram engines were ordered in July 1883 with two more in September and the service began as soon as the first engine was delivered on 22nd October 1883. In total, 16 engines were supplied by the firm of Black Hawthorn & Co while most of the actual passenger cars were built by the Falcon Engine & Car Co. These originally had open top decks but, as passengers emerged frequently covered in smuts and were always at risk from burning cinders, they were quickly covered over.

Although more routes had originally been planned, only three routes were actually constructed. The first ran to Heworth via the High Street, Sunderland Road and Felling station; the second to Low Fell via the High Street, The Crescent and Sunderland Road, whilst the last route ran to the Teams area of Gateshead via Mulgrave Terrace and Askew Road. Altogether, about six miles of standard gauge tramway was built – mostly using a single track with passing loops.

Steam tram no 5 on the High Street. Built 1883/4 by the Falcon Engine & Car Co.

All routes ran a 20 minute service with a maximum fare of 2d. Not just people were carried on the trams – livestock could also travel and between midnight and 5 am, the cars had yet another use as they could be used to convey refuse and road material. The Low Fell trams had their own coke store at the junction of Kells Lane and Durham Road, the other trams refuelled at the Sunderland Road depot.

A Lancaster built tram car passing 53 High Street.

The last two Gateshead tramcars were built by the Lancaster Carriage and Wagon Co in 1889. These had an enclosed top deck with transverse seats but were difficult to see in the dark as the cars were lit by oil lamps fixed to the bulkheads.

Gateshead became the last town in the North East to convert their tramway to electric traction. Work started in June 1900 and while the work was being carried out, the steam trams continued to run. However, their service was necessarily limited and 1900 saw a £372 loss in revenue. This time, new, longer tramways were constructed and some of the existing tramways were converted to double track. The official opening took place on 8th May 1901 when a tram carrying a large number of local dignitaries travelled up the High Street to Felling and Heworth, returning via Sunderland Road. That evening saw the final journeys of the old steam trams with most of them ending their days rather ignominiously in Hind's scrapyard at Park Lane.

A no 47 Milnes tram constructed in 1902 at Shipcote. This was made in Germany and had a lever slipper brake. Note the nice advert for 'Holloway's Pills & Ointment'.

Next day, the new electric trams began operating. Forty-five electric tramcars were ordered for the new service which proved such an instant success that five more were quickly ordered. It wasn't just the trams that were different. There were now specified stopping points on the route – the old days of hailing a tram had disappeared – and this speeded up travelling times. Ticket prices too were cheaper, with a standard penny fare regardless of the distance travelled. However, this did not make economic sense on the three mile uphill route to Wrekenton and so from 1910, a novel 'fair fare' system was introduced on that route only, of a farthing per stopping point.

During the First World War, female tram conductresses became a common sight on the trams as more and more men were called up (*see page 101*). Life on the trams went on very much as usual during this period apart from one major incident.

Right: This picture shows Rose Vanner, the first lady tram conductress (shown here in her own clothes rather than uniform). Rose went on to become Gateshead's first lady tram inspector and was the daughter of Walter Vanner (see page 61).

The 'overturning of a tramcar'

The picture below shows the most serious accident involving a tram in Gateshead. The time was 7 pm, the date was 5th February 1916 and the number 7 tram had just left the Bensham terminus for Gateshead. At that time, this route was single track. As it reached the Ravensworth Hotel (now the Bensham Jockey), the driver, a young man called Leonard George Jane, saw a stationary tram ahead. He put on his hand brake and waited for a signal from the other driver. Nothing happened but a young man walking down the bank stopped and told Jane that a fight had broken out on the other tram. Jane decided to walk up the hill to investigate. Unfortunately, he omitted to tell his young conductress. Nor did he apply the track brake. While the tram was stationary, more people began to board it and due to the extra weight, the tram became unstable. The

The no 7 tram partly covered in tarpaulin. The photograph was probably taken the day following the accident.

situation worsened when the conductress, realising there were too many on board tried to get people to leave. At this point, the tram slowly began to run downhill picking up speed as it did so. It ran backwards for almost 200 yards before finally overturning onto a plot of vacant land on the curve at the end of Saltwell Road.

When Jane eventually returned to his vehicle he was met by an appalling sight. A crowd had gathered around the tram and people were frantically trying to remove those travellers trapped inside. A number of passengers had severe injuries including the conductress who had a fractured leg, but there were no passenger fatalities. However, the tram had overturned onto a father, mother and their seven year old son and a young serviceman home on leave and walking to the cinema, all of whom were killed instantly.

The inquest was held three days later and a verdict was given that *'the deceased were accidentally crushed through the overturning of a tramcar which ran away, owing to the additional weight of passengers, during the temporary absence of the driver.'*

The following day Jane was charged with causing the deaths of four people and remanded on bail. However, it transpired that he had not had proper training (in peacetime he would have been too young to drive a tram), had seen the company's rules but had not read them and had no notion that a track brake should have been applied as well as the hand brake. One month later, the charge was thrown out by the grand jury at Durham Quarter Sessions.

The tram was eventually rebuilt as an eight window body and curved roof with seats for 32 and came back into service, still as the number 7 in 1920. However, within a few years it changed its number to 52 and ran on the Teams route until 1951. It became the last working four wheeled single deck passenger tram to operate in the British Isles.

The photo left shows it in the Windy Nook garden of an ex tram driver in September 1959. It was later sent to Crich Museum of Transport and has recently been further restored and can now be seen at Beamish.

No 52 (formerly no 7) Gateshead's last single decker.

1920 saw a general price rise and new fares were introduced which would remain unchanged for the next 30 years. Incidentally, dogs could be carried on the trams for payment of a penny providing they did not cause offence to other passengers!

The next major development came when the High Level Bridge was strengthened to take trams and a through service began operating between Newcastle and Gateshead. Work began in June 1922 on the approaches to the bridges and lasted until mid-November when the bridge was closed to all traffic while the rails were laid. The new tramway was formally opened on 12th January 1923 (*below*) and in the first two days it was estimated that 90,000 fares were taken. Eight new through services began operating with a penny fare which included a halfpenny toll for each passenger. The new service was an immediate success and soon became one of the busiest tramways in the British Isles.

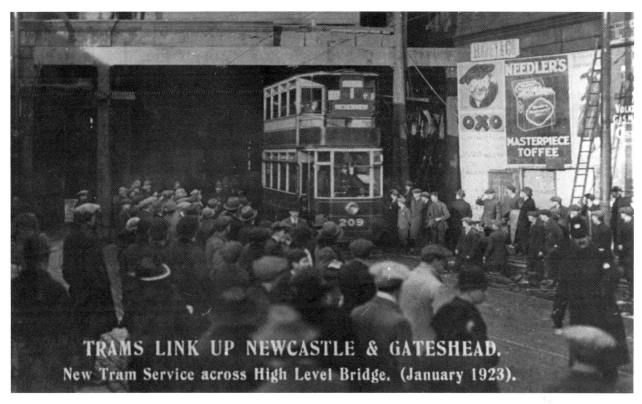

TRAMS LINK UP NEWCASTLE & GATESHEAD.
New Tram Service across High Level Bridge. (January 1923).

Before the High Level was strengthened, the only public passenger service to operate on the road deck was the 'Ha'penny Lop'. This was a horse brake with a halfpenny fare which was a source of some annoyance as foot travellers crossing the bridge had to pay a halfpenny each, whilst the brake, which could carry 40 passengers, only paid fourpence.

Nothing could be done however and the horse brake survived until June 1931.

The tram service finally came to an end in Gateshead on 4th August 1951 although bus services had been gradually replacing trams on some routes for a few years previously. Newcastle had been converting to trolley buses since 1934 and Gateshead were on course to do the same. The outbreak of war however, stopped any plans for conversion and, as a result of the blackout, resulted in Gateshead's only tram extension since the tracks were laid in 1901, when the

The horse brake with the Wellington Street branch of Gateshead Co-operative Society in the background.

Low Fell terminus was extended by a few yards to negate the difficulties of the junction between Kells Lane, Chowdene Bank and Durham Road in the dark.

After the war, trams continued to run successfully in Gateshead but their days were numbered. By the end of the war, Gateshead Council had decided that the town was now too congested with traffic for trolley buses to be successful and instead decided to convert within two years to a motor bus system.

One of the last trams on Pine Street, 4th August 1951.

The first bus service was introduced between Wrekenton and Heworth on 5th March 1950 with others soon following. The 4th August 1951 became a momentous day in Gateshead's transport history as this was the last day that the trams ran. The photo above shows a Dunston tram in Pine Street on that day. The very last service tram, no 20, left Newcastle Central Station at 11.00 pm packed with passengers – many of them making one last sentimental journey. The tram was followed by the official last tram, no 16, containing officials of the British Electric Traction Company, Gateshead & District Omnibus Company, Newcastle Corporation Transport and a number of civic dignitaries from both sides of the river. The car passed along Askew Road and Pine Street through streets packed with spectators, many of them putting coins on the lines to be flattened by the trams and kept as souvenirs. Both trams reversed at Gateshead Station and ran to Sunderland Road depot which was specially decorated with bunting for the occasion. The

Removing the tracks on Gateshead High Street.

subsequent removal of the tram lines was speedy and within two years, no traces remained. The final stretch removed was that on the High Street. It was estimated that a total weight of 3,000 tons of tram track were lifted.

Most of the tram cars were sold for scrap but some single deck bodies were sold to individuals. Four of these were used as farm

Four balcony trams wait to be scrapped at Sunderland Road depot.

buildings in Northumberland on land between Felton and Alnwick. Nineteen were sold complete to the Grimsby and Immingham Electric Railway although one of these was damaged during transport and never used.

Buses (run by the tramways company) had co-existed with the trams but originally only as a 'tram extension' from the tram terminus at Low Fell to Chester-le-Street. They had been running from May 1913 when it had been decided that a tramway extension was not economically viable. Nine buses with 30 hp engines were ordered with a through fare from the High Level Bridge to Chester-le-Street of sixpence. Each bus could seat 16 people inside and 18 outside. The success of this service led to the creation of Northern General Transport Limited in November 1913. Ten years later, in January 1923, they opened a new waiting room at the Low Fell tram terminus. Whilst this had formerly been the bus terminus as well, the company now extended their route and created a new terminus outside the railway bridge on Gateshead High Street. From here they ran a half hourly service to Durham with a journey time of 90 minutes. A former coal depot which faced Gateshead West station was converted to a bus station at the same time.

A driver and his conductor proudly pose outside their bus.

Driving in Gateshead has always been a challenge from the rutted and frequently muddy turnpike roads of the 18th and early 19th centuries to the temporary 'one way' system which operated in 1966. Today a series of traffic lights and roundabouts can still cause confusion to the unwary traveller but have largely succeeded in easing congestion and improved traffic flow, even if the viaduct built in 1971 has rather too successfully steered traffic away from

A 1960s postcard of the new A1 road roundabout!

the centre of town to the dismay of its shopkeepers.

The first real traffic problems were probably caused by the steam trams with one of the worst spots for incidents being the bottom of West Street. Several different tram routes terminated here and by 1907 conditions were giving serious cause for concern. West Street was eventually widened at its southern end, but the northern end remained a traffic bottleneck for years. As the numbers of motorised vehicles began to increase, solutions had to be found and in 1931 motorists were faced with 'traffic robots' for the first time. These new traffic lights were installed at the Gateshead end of the Tyne Bridge and replaced the policemen who had formerly been on point duty there. A contemporary newspaper report commented *'Let us hope that Gateshead's pedestrians will ... acknowledge the winking signals of the robots.'* They proved a success and soon a further five sets of traffic lights were installed with the help of a grant from the Ministry of Transport.

However, even traffic lights couldn't compensate for the inconvenience caused when the Swing Bridge was in operation as can be seen in the photograph below taken at 11.24 am on 22nd May 1924. The backlog of traffic could cause long delays and was the cause of frequent complaints.

Traffic backlog on Bridge Street. The Full Moon public house is on the right of the photograph.

Driving down Gateshead High Street became particularly hazardous at the north end as the photograph above shows. At the junction of Bottle Bank and Church Street the signpost proclaims on one side' Danger' and on the other side 'To Newcastle'.

On 1st June 1933, an accident occurred in West Street which made newspaper headlines and caption editors happy. Described as '*A Run on the Bank*' this was caused by a 10 ton lorry carrying Australian meat which spectacularly crashed into Barclay's Bank (formerly the Mechanics Institute) due to brake failure. The building survived to tell the tale although it was eventually demolished in 1972.

On Coronation Day, 12th May 1937, tolls were removed from the High Level and the Redheugh Bridges. This resulted in an immediate increase in road traffic, with Sunderland Road being described as the heaviest traffic road in the county. In 1938, plans for a new road (which became the Felling by-pass) were drawn up, with the Ministry of Transport offering a grant of £152,000 and expected to be implemented the following year. However, the outbreak of war effectively put these plans on hold and work on the bypass would not begin until the late 1950s.

A Run on The Bank in Gateshead

Australia makes an impression.

49

More cars of course meant more petrol stations and Beacon Garage (now Kwik-Fit at Low Fell) was just one of them. On the right, Willie Moon, the proprietor, is serving petrol.

A temporary one way system was introduced in 1966 preparatory to the building of the new viaduct systems designed by Ove Arup. This was essential as traffic in Gateshead was now causing a real problem

The multi-storey car park (*below*) was designed to house the many motorists who were confidently expected to arrive in Gateshead to do their shopping. This cost £200,000 and was capable of housing 500 vehicles –certainly an optimistic estimate as

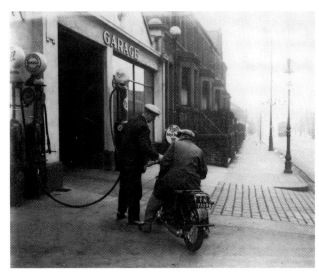

car ownership in Gateshead at this time was one of the lowest in the country. The car park was in trouble almost from the start. Meant to open by Christmas 1968, it was delayed until 2nd August 1969 as cracks appeared in the concrete and these had to be rectified. It was meant to provide '*a significant stimulus to town centre trade.*' It never did however, as the subsequent new flyover built in 1971 was responsible for completely bypassing Gateshead and taking shoppers direct to Newcastle. The car park was planned

with a restaurant on the top floor – however, this never opened and remained as a constant reminder of failed hopes for the future.

In 1971, the car park had to close for a couple of months for reinforcement and in 1994, the top storeys were permanently closed.

The car park achieved fame and a degree of notoriety when it was featured in *Get Carter* the 1971 film starring Michael Caine but it was never really regarded with any degree of affection and when the car park eventually closed in 2008 most people looked forward to its eventual demolition. Sadly for the architect Owen Luder, he had to see yet another of his iconic buildings (there were others elsewhere) demolished to make way for the construction of yet another new shopping centre.

An alternative to walking, if you didn't have or want to use mechanised transport was cycling which became popular in Gateshead towards the end of the 19th century. One of the best known cyclists was George Brown, who bought his first bicycle in 1889 for £2 10s (*see page 83*). In 1897 he recorded a personal mileage of 1,750 miles! He also formed the Gateshead and District Motor Club.

And finally ... a vehicle often used for group outings in the 1920s and 1930s – the ubiquitous charabanc.

Chapter Five
Shop 'til You Drop

Shopping in Gateshead centred around the High Street (once known as the Fore Street – and originally just a simple track which led down to the river Tyne), at one time estimated to be the longest High Street in England as until the Tyne Bridge was built, it ran right down to the Quayside encompassing Bottle Bank.

Whellan's 1895 trade directory lists 28 provision dealers, 21 butchers, 17 pubs, 4 breweries, 9 grocers, 7 flour dealers, 7 hairdressers, 6 tailors, 6 fruiterers, 5 haberdashers, 4 milliners and 4 confectioners. Nineteenth century shoppers in Gateshead were certainly spoilt for choice!

Originally houses were built on either side but later they were converted to business premises with gardens which were in turn replaced by 'dry quays'. These were flagged platforms raised some feet above the footpath so that goods could easily be unloaded onto them. One of the quays can be seen in this photograph on the right taken in 1886 of one of the oldest parts of the High Street and shows the junction with Jackson Street. Not long after this photograph was taken, these shops were demolished and the Metropole Theatre (*see also page 93*) was built on the site.

A family shopping on the High Street in the 1890s. A steam tram can be seen in the background.

From left to right: clogger W. Jones, joiner R. Millican and hay and straw dealer William Atkinson.

The shops shown on the photograph left were lower down the High Street on the east side. Outside Preston's the brushmaker's (established in 1850), the symbol of a boar can be seen. This was a sign to the illiterate that this shop sold brushes (represented by the bristles of the boar). The sign was removed in the 1920s. Colliers Clay Pipe factory was above Preston's with the footwear shop of Andrew Gaddes on the left and Scott & Crow blacksmiths on the other. Underneath Scott & Crow's was the entrance to Plough Yard.

Another shop which had a sign outside its door was William Hunter's tobacconists (*right*). He had brought this six foot tall carved oak figure of a Highlander from the Quayside and it stood outside his little shop for over 100 years before being sent, rather appropriately, to Edinburgh.

Until the late 19th century, there were no shops south of Park Lane but then this area too was developed with a variety of small shops. Among these were Dietz the pork butchers and Laws Herbal Stores. Dietz were one of numerous German pork butchers who, with their families, came to England in the latter years of the 19th century, but unlike many of their fellow citizens, they did not anglicise their names. Around 1900 they took over O.J. Burns' pork butcher's shop. Dietz, with their distinctive cream tiled frontage, had plenty of competition – in 1915 there were six butchers shops between numbers 265-305 High Street!

Laws Herbal Stores was one of the last 'unique' Gateshead shops and was patronised by those wanting the famous sarsaparilla (brewed to a secret recipe) and also Laws' pineapple punch. The shop can be seen on the extreme right of the photograph left, taken on 12th June 1971.

Another herbalist was F.W. Bernard, nicknamed 'the Low Fell giant' who had a shop lower down the High Street.

As well as herbalists there were numerous chemists shops. One of the earliest was Beatton's Half Moon Pharmacy situated at the junction of Half Moon Lane and the High Street. The photo left, taken about 1900, shows it advertising 'Glendinning's beef & malt wine for invalids'.

There were also a number of boot and shoe shops and one of the longest established was Knotts. In 1886, Joseph Armstrong Knott opened a leather merchants shop at

197 High Street. He added footwear when slippers were received in lieu of cash from Tyneside slipper and clog manufacturers who, due to the depression, could only pay in kind. Over the next 60 years, business flourished in five different premises, all within 200 yards of each other. When one of their old shops closed, they let it for the remainder of its lease to a 'fat woman' exhibition, much to the consternation of the landlord.

Other specialist stores included Wilkes furniture store. This was a three storey shop which was destroyed by fire on 2nd May 1953. Seven units of the Newcastle and Gateshead fire brigades fought the flames. However, whilst the store did not survive, the grocer's and wallpaper shops on either side were saved. Wilkes was later rebuilt.

Bywell's furniture shop opened in 1936 opposite the junction of High Street and Sunderland Road (now O'Keefe's public house). Owned by Wilfred Bransky, this firm had an extensive hire purchase business. They also had premises on Warwick Street and Coatsworth Road.

Larger stores included: Gillies music store, Hedleys the drapers, Bon Marché, and From Weaver to Wearer. Easily one of the most stylish frontages belonged to Doggarts store which closed in 1970 at the time the photograph on the right was taken. (The notice in the window states 'termination of business'.) It was then taken over by John Blundell, drapers, and following their demise, for a number of years was occupied by KwikSave.

An earlier building on the same site can be seen on page 72 when it was the premises of Christopher Heap, flour merchant. This building was demolished when it, and the land surrounding it, was bought by William Young, son of Charley Young – one of Gateshead's most successful butchers. Charley had opened his first shop on Pine Street at the turn of the 20th century and within 30 years he had 34 branches. Young's made a variety of products including meat pies, sausages and potted meat. They also had a poultry department and a kosher food preparing department. Young's built their manufacturing premises behind the site of Heap's (the site of which they sold to Doggarts) and had their main butcher's shop next door.

Another interesting frontage belonged to Younghusband's (*see photo left*), situated at 29 High Street, an area which was demolished in the mid 1920s to make way for the construction of the new Tyne Bridge approach road. On their frontage was displayed Gateshead's coat of arms. This was completely legal as Gateshead had inadvertently forgotten to register their coat of arms with the Court of Heralds! But Gateshead was always renowned for two main shops – Snowball's and Shephard's. Snowball's was often referred to as 'the Harrods of the north' and it truly seemed as if you could buy or order virtually anything from this store.

Snowball's

In 1850 William Snowball set up a small drapers business in Gateshead. This proved successful so, in 1866, the firm moved to extensive and elaborate new premises at the north end of the High Street on the site of the Black Bull, a former coaching inn. They called their new premises Kent House and with a ground floor area of nearly one acre and with the store extending 400 feet from the High Street to Oakwellgate, they supplied a huge variety of items including linoleum – the new floor covering of the Victorian age. (Both William and his brother James were among the original shareholders in the world's first linoleum factory at Staines.) By 1887, Snowball's were employing about 200 staff.

They were an enterprising firm. As well as supplying tents for outdoor events, they supplied the original cocoa matting for the Town Hall as well as kitchens, bedding, carpets, mantel making, upholstering, and polishing. Their sales were noteworthy and attracted huge crowds. They also looked after their staff, giving them statutory half days as well as organising outings, sports and other events for them.

In 1886, Snowball's became the first shop in the North East to install a patent cash railway which was described as *'the greatest invention and wonder of the age'* and so innovative that it was deemed worthy of a special 'launch' by the Mayor of Gateshead who sent the first cash ball rolling on its 650 feet journey to the cashier's desk.

One of Snowball's delivery vans.

A cabinet furniture shop was added to their already extensive premises in 1903 and, as the 20th century dawned, it seemed that Snowball's were set for even further success and expansion. They might be with us still were it not for the construction of the Tyne Bridge which began in August 1925. In the way of the northbound roadway was Snowball's 'Kent House'. A compulsory purchase order was issued and the front section of the store was demolished with a new frontage being built about 30 yards back on Church Street.

However, whilst the new bridge was successful, (despite the comic remark at the time that it would never last, as it was built on the Sandhill on one side and Snowball's on the other!), the store failed to thrive and eventually closed during the Second World War. You can see another photograph of the store when temporarily used by Shephard's on the following page.

Once Snowball's closed, Shephard's took over the mantle of Gateshead's best shopping attraction.

This photograph was taken in 1925, shortly before the enforced alterations to the store.

Shephard's

Emerson Shephard opened a boot and shoe shop in the front room of a small house in Swinburne Street in 1906 with only a few pounds, one assistant and 500 pairs of boots and shoes. This proved so successful that, two years later, he moved to premises on the

corner of West Street and Ellison Street which he gradually extended. By 1924 he had added a drapery department and had 10 other shops (*see photograph on page 61*).

By the Second World War, his premises (which had been extended in 1934) covered 100,000 square feet along Ellison Street, 11 more branches had been opened and the store had over 560 employees. Like Snowball's, Shephard's were a good firm to work for and in 1936 they established a staff pension scheme.

On the 18th January 1946, disaster struck when one of Tyneside's worst fires destroyed not only all the main premises but all the stock. It was said that the heat from the fire was so fierce that it blistered the varnish on the front doors in nearby Nelson Street. However, Emerson Shephard did not give up. Literally within a few hours, 'the guv'nor' as he was always affectionately known, had organised temporary facilities and soon the store re-opened in Kent House – previous home of Snowball's.

A lesser man than Shephard might have settled for this, but

Shephard's Ellison Street store in 1927.

Bystanders watch as the fire takes hold.

almost immediately he began planning a new store which sadly, he did not live to see as he died the year before it opened. The new store opened, on the site of the old one, on 9th

March 1951. The temporary premises were closed for five days so that all the goods could be transferred. It cost £200,000 and was opened by Emerson Shephard's daughter. The whole of the store was designed with huge windows and skylights to make artificial light almost unnecessary and it was decorated in what were described as tasteful shades of peach and grey. The pride of the new store was the first floor fashion department.

Shephard's temporary store in the former Snowball's shop in 1950.

Above: Shephard's travelling van.

Right: A Shephard's advert from the 1960s.

Left: A five shilling Shephard's coin.

Shephard's had their own money which could only be spent in the store. This was popular with the poor who couldn't afford to buy goods in the shops so used the ticket men who collected money door-to-door from households. This was then exchanged for a ticket, which in turn was changed to 'Shephard's Money'. This developed a black market all of its own with Shephard's money often sold in public houses for well below its face value in real cash terms.

Shephard's had their own advertising song in the 1960s which many people still fondly remember.

'Shephard's of Gateshead
The biggest and the best store
Shephard's of Gateshead
Have what you're looking for
There's so much to see and the car park is free
Come shopping at Shephard's for the whole family'

Above: Shephard's new store. The space in front of it would later be occupied by Tesco's.

In 1980, Shephard's finally disappeared from Gateshead with the store being bought by Tesco's and renamed Shopping City. Sadly this enterprise too failed and the shop was demolished in 1986, subsequently becoming the site of Tesco's car park.

Right: Gateshead's short lived 'Shopping City' with Gateshead's first piece of public art sculpture Sports Day (1986) in the foreground. (Photograph by Trevor Ermel.)

The only other shop of any significance in Gateshead to rival either Snowball's or Shephard's was the Co-operative Society. This began in the former rectory in Oakwellgate in 1861 before moving to a railway arch in Wellington Street. Before long, four railway arches were being used by the store and the Co-op had also acquired a steam flour mill in Maiden's Walk. They opened their first branch in Askew Road in 1877 and added a second in the High Street two years later.

However, their new central premises were opened in Jackson Street in 1884 – premises which had an ornate pediment with the symbols of a beehive. This was a symbol often used by the Co-op and signified the importance of co-operation – one bee alone could not survive but in a group co-operating it would.

Within a few years, branches had been established at Low Fell (1887), Wrekenton (1891) and Teams (1892), a coal depot was established at Shearlegs Road to which stables were added in 1904 and dairying was in place at the rear of Jackson Street in 1907. From an initial membership of 210 in 1863, by 1905 the Society had 11,782 members and to celebrate the Society's golden jubilee in Gateshead in 1911, a cot was endowed at the Children's Hospital on Dryden Road (*see page 65*) at a cost of £500.

The 1925 Co-op building is the tallest building shown here – neatly sandwiched between the original shop and New Century House built in 1964.

By 1925 there were 18 branches throughout Gateshead and a new store in Jackson Street was built in an Art Deco style, described by the Co-op as '*an imposing pile of masonry which reflects high degree of credit upon the Society*.' It had a frontage of 98 feet and a depth of 90 feet. Opening this store meant that furnishing, shoes and the drapery could all be expanded. The façade was faced with stone from Windy Nook quarries and the shop fronts were constructed of bronzed metal.

The premises were further expanded when New Century House opened in 1964 on the site of the former Mill Inn at the top of Jackson Street. Sadly, these buildings closed in 2007.

Despite all these shops however, the High Street often had a neglected look. A

New Century House and Jackson Street in 1967.

reporter describing the area in 1949 said '*There is a slatternly look about the streets and shops ... the whole place is a vast desert of decay ... it is doubtful if I will find a grimmer dirtier town during all my tour*' while a Gateshead Councillor, speaking two years earlier proclaimed '*We are faced today with a street which is in a dilapidated and distressing state*.'

In 1959, construction of the Felling bypass and the new roundabout at the north end of the High Street resulted in the demolition of a number of shops. It was about this time that the idea of developing a new town centre was beginning to be discussed. Original ideas included a theatre and cinema, a nursery and electrically heated walkways but these never happened. In 1961, Gateshead Council signed a one million pound deal with Millerdale Properties of Newcastle with the design of the new centre going to the Owen Luder partnership. This practice was concentrating on the then modern 'Brutalist' school

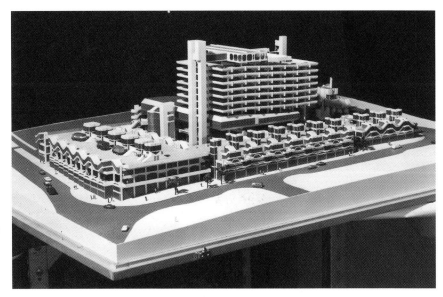

of architecture – a style signified by plain blocks of reinforced concrete. A model of the shopping centre costing £150 went on show at the Town Hall and was also part of the Royal Academy's Summer Exhibition in London (*right*). Optimistically anticipating that the development would be completed in 1963, it was confidently stated that the town was '*expected to have one of the most advanced shopping centres in Europe.*' However, 1963 proved to be a trifle optimistic as work did not begin until 1965 when earth and rock was dug out for the foundations. Finally, three years later in 1968, the new pedestrianized precinct, complete with canopies, covered walkways and 52 shops plus three department stores opened. However, three years after opening, only 15 out of 50 shop units were occupied, a total of 30 cars were occupying just a few of the many spaces in the car park and a report in the Journal in January 1971 stated '*A cold wind buffeted against the grey concrete of Gateshead's towering shopping precinct yesterday and whistled through the many empty shop units.*' In an effort to improve matters, it was announced that an indoor market hall would be built – the first general market to be held in the town since the mid 16th century. However, once the new A1 viaduct opened in 1971 effectively bypassing the town centre, trade slumped.

One of the stores which had opened in the new precinct was Presto's supermarket, opened by the comedian Norman Vaughan in December 1968. One of its main selling points was the introduction of conveyor belts at checkouts, and their store slogan was '*Every buy a bargain.*' The store was described as '*Gateshead's bangest-up-to-date supermarket.*' However, within three years, the store had to close for two months while

reinforcements were made to the building when test borings revealed that the ground beneath Trinity Square was riddled with mine workings.

Tesco opened their supermarket in November 1972 and it was then their largest single storey supermarket in the country. It cost £361,000, covered 57,000 square feet and their food hall was claimed to be the largest in Britain. In 1975, the store was extended to two floors although was soon reduced to one floor of retail. In response to demand, the store introduced home freezer packs in 1974 – a two pound bag of chips cost 29p. To cater for the rising numbers of people enjoying wine on their holidays abroad, Tesco's sold cut price wine at 69p per litre! Forty-one years later Tesco's was demolished for a complete rebuild as part of the new Trinity Square development.

Other shopping in central Gateshead was concentrated on West Street but there were a variety of smaller shops such as the one belonging to Mrs Walker pictured left, outside her little shop on Ellison Street. Mrs Walker appears to be advertising the 'Compliments of the Season'. As well as shops, there were tea and coffee rooms such as those owned by

Liddell confectioners at 83 High West Street (*right*).

Outside of the town centre, Askew Road for the Teams area, Coatsworth Road for Saltwell and Bensham and Durham Road for Low Fell provided thriving smaller areas. All had branches of the Co-op plus a variety of smaller shops including branches of Gateshead's first supermarket – Laws stores.

The first Walter Willson store in Gateshead was based at Low Fell – surprisingly late as Mr Willson himself was Mayor of Gateshead in the 19th century at a time when he had no shops in the town. However, Walter Willson's pulled off a remarkable advertising 'coup' in 1930 when they claimed to be the first firm in Britain and possibly the world to advertise by airship. The 80hp airship was 157 feet long, and could travel at a maximum speed of 75 miles per hour.

'*Walter Willson's on top' was the slogan which could be observed by anyone in the North East in June 1930.*

Another Low Fell shop was this one which belonged to stationer Fred Robinson (*shown below in 1903*). One of the many products he sold was postcards – the essential means of communication in the early 20th century. Many were supplied by the firm of R. Johnston who had his main shop at 27 West Street (*see photo overleaf*), popularly known as 'The Bible depot'. Johnston's first shop opened on West Street in 1877 before moving to new premises also in the same street. Sadly, this shop with all the machinery was destroyed in the disastrous Shephard's fire of 1946.

R. Johnston's shop, 27 West Street.
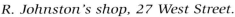
Costelloe's around 1921.

New premises were opened at 73 West Street but as all the negatives (over 14,000) from which the postcards were produced had been destroyed, the shop had to diversify and offered fancy goods for sale as well as stationery.

Pawnbrokers of course could be found everywhere. One of the main firms was Costelloe's at 80 Prince Consort Road. Built about 1867, the building was demolished about 1972. Like Walter Willson, William Costelloe was also a Mayor of Gateshead. Other branches were based at Redheugh and Sunderland Road.

The premises shown here on the right are those of George R. Brown, described as 'Purveyor of Cycles & Motors & Radio Gramophones.' The photo underneath shows Brown's carnival float advertising 'His Master's Voice' gramophone records. Both photographs date from the 1930s.

Coatsworth Road, originally known as Union Lane, provided shops of all description. At the time when the photograph below was taken there were bootmakers, grocers, drapers, a photographer's, post office, laundry and three public houses.

A busy Coatsworth Road at the turn of the 20th century. The Honeysuckle public house can be seen at the right of the photograph.

While Gateshead High Street has been redeveloped twice, and now looks unrecognisable from earlier photographs, with many of the older buildings demolished and those remaining being masked by new buildings, Coatsworth Road has changed little in the way of appearance and the variety of shops on offer today are remarkably similar to those of 100 years ago.

One form of shopping which has largely disappeared from our

A branch of Shephard's at 21 Coatsworth Road.

streets is the travelling van or shop. At one time, butchers, bakers, fish sellers and even chemists could be seen out and about in Gateshead. One of the best known was that of Walter Vanner, popularly referred to as 'Vanner the fishman' who hawked his fish around, firstly with a horse and cart and then a motor car.

However, the rise of online shopping means that we still see supermarket delivery vans – but how many people know that this all first began here in Gateshead in 1981 with a tele-shopping service for elderly people (using teletext) based at Sunderland Road Library through a partnership of Gateshead Social Services and Tesco.

Chapter Six
Coughs and Sneezes Spread Diseases

Today, Gateshead has numerous facilities to help its residents stay healthy but this hasn't always been the case. Even in the early 20th century, Gateshead was regarded as an unhealthy town to live in. When, as a young woman, Sister Winifred Laver (who went on to found the Vine Street Mission) first proposed travelling to Gateshead, she was firmly told by her doctor that if she did so, she would not last a year. In the 19th century, Gateshead had one of the highest death rates in the country and had the dubious distinction of being regarded as the tuberculosis capital of England. Well into the 20th century, TB continued to be a killer in the town.

Much of the problem was caused by the overcrowding and unhealthy conditions in which the bulk of Gateshead's population were forced to occupy. Until the early 19th century, there were regular outbreaks of plague (including the Black Death in the 14th century and the wonderfully named 'Jolly rant' of the 17th century) but in December 1831, Gateshead residents found a new disease in their midst. It was not long before the word 'cholera' was on everyone's lips. In three days, 27th, 28th and 29th December, John Collinson, Gateshead's Rector, and his curates buried 48 cholera victims. Collinson later took the unusual step of erecting, in St Edmund's churchyard, a memorial to 222 cholera victims of the 1831/2 epidemic who were buried there. The memorial bears the inscription *'In the midst of life we are in death. Watch therefore for ye know not what hour your Lord doth come,'* – which is an apt biblical quotation, as cholera, the cause of which was then unknown, could strike without warning and kill within 24 hours.

John Collinson, Rector of Gateshead 1810-40.

This outbreak spurred John Collinson and William Henry Brockett, a businessman and political activist, to take action and on 3rd February 1832, (when Gateshead was still in the grip of the disease) a meeting was held in the Anchorage School at St Mary's Church, attended by *'most of the respectable inhabitants of the Borough.'* The result was the Dispensary, founded with the aim *'To give financial assistance in ameliorating and preserving the public health by placing medicine and advice within the reach of the poor.'* Money was raised by one guinea subscriptions which allowed the donor to receive seven dispensary letters. These could be given to anyone who was sick who would then be given preferential treatment at the Dispensary. Other 'non-letter' cases were also treated but had to wait their turn.

The Dispensary lasted until the formation of the National Health Service in 1948, with much of its funding supported by legacies which allowed it to pay for doctors and nursing. For much of its existence, it was dealing with diseases caused through sub-standard living conditions and it was to be sorely tested during two further outbreaks of cholera in 1849 and 1853 and again when treating the many injuries of those affected by the Great Fire in 1854. The original building was found to be

The Dispensary, Nelson Street.

too small and eventually moved to new premises in Nelson Street, purchased from the solicitor (and soon to be Town Clerk) Joseph Willis Swinburne. The Dispensary's resources were to be tested again during the 20th century due largely to outbreaks of the Spanish Flu – a pandemic which particularly affected the healthy, rather than the young, elderly or infirm. In two weeks during November 1918, 63 people died as a result of Spanish Flu in Gateshead. This resulted in a rise in patient numbers and a record was set in 1919, when 17,186 patients were treated at the Dispensary. By 1937, however, financial support for the Dispensary was dwindling and only 20 residents were actively subscribing to it. By then, the premises were regarded as out of date and although plans were produced for a new building, it was never built.

The Dispensary treated patients for disease but Oakwellgate baths and washhouses were built in 1855 in a conscious effort to help improve hygiene in Gateshead. These were not swimming baths but individual baths – hot water could be supplied for sixpence or cold water for tuppence. But this was still too expensive for the poor and so the baths weren't well used. The washhouses, where clothes could be washed, however, were much better patronised at a cost of 1d an hour – in the early days 400 people a week were using them. The baths and washhouses closed in the early 20th century and, until its eventual destruction by fire in 1986, the building had a variety of uses.

For most of the 19th century, other than the Dispensary, there was no public hospital in Gateshead, although the workhouse had its own small sick ward built in 1854 after two rooms had been converted to house cholera victims during the second outbreak of the disease in 1849.

Oakwellgate baths and washhouses towards the end of its life when used as a warehouse.

In 1880, Sheriff Hill Isolation Hospital was opened in a conscious effort to get infection away from the overcrowded slums. The hospital site covered four acres and, to give a clear 'keep away' message, was surrounded by a stone wall topped with broken glass and barbed wire. The hospital had 38 beds, later increased to 64 in 1900. When severe outbreaks of smallpox broke out, Sheriff Hill became 'smallpox only', with patients suffering from other infectious diseases sent to Saltwell Hall (now demolished) which was used for a time as an extra isolation hospital.

In the first three years of the hospital opening, there were 248 cases of typhus and 504 cases of smallpox recorded in Gateshead. Some of the patients were sent to the Isolation Hospital at Sheriff Hill where all four nurses and the matron (comprising the whole of the nursing staff at that time) promptly contracted typhus.

Whilst it was thought that isolating smallpox cases at Sheriff Hill was the proper way to treat the disease, a report written following a major outbreak in 1903/4 suggested that the disease was most prevalent in houses situated within a mile of the hospital suggesting that the infection was being carried on the wind. Following this epidemic, 4,847 vaccinations and 5,240 re-vaccinations were carried out by the Gateshead Board of Guardians. Despite this however, further severe outbreaks of smallpox and typhus occurred in 1907 and 1910.

By the 20th century, awareness of the importance of improving public health in Gateshead was rising, and gradually, due largely to slum clearances, the situation began to improve. However, there were still severe outbreaks of scarlet fever during 1933-35 and outbreaks of diphtheria between 1936 and 1946. Gateshead had the unenviable record of having the highest death rate in the country for whooping cough in 1936.

Tuberculosis too, was still a constant problem. In 1920 the Council bought Greenesfield

House from the North Eastern Railway for £3,000 to use as a TB dispensary and it opened the following year. In June 1926, Whinney House Hospital, which had served as a Voluntary Aid Detachment (VAD) hospital during the First World War (*see page 103*), opened as a tuberculosis hospital with 48 beds, 10 wards and reception rooms.

In a further effort to combat the disease, Gateshead TB Care Committee was established in Gladstone Terrace. By 1936, Gateshead had dropped from first to third place in the TB deaths league table – this was a welcome step in the right direction, but still wasn't good enough. Anti-tubercular injections (BCG) were trialled during 1955 and proved successful with an annual vaccination programme operating thereafter. Between April-June 1956, a major mass screening programme was seen in Gateshead with five mobile sites being used and by 1962, James Grant, the Medical Officer of Health, could confidently report that there had been no deaths due to TB and only six cases in children reported the previous year.

The Mayor and Mayoress at Whinney House Hospital distributing Easter eggs to patients on 8th April 1939.

Greenesfield Health Centre on Mulgrave Terrace opened in 1938 at a cost of £16,048. This largely replaced Greenesfield House although the latter still retained its TB clinic.

In the late 1930s, plans were drawn up for a major new hospital estimated to cost £293,000 and for modernisation of the Infectious Diseases hospital at a cost of £70,000. The foundation stone was laid in September 1939 by Alderman Peter Strong Hancock (Deputy Mayor and Chairman of the Health & Sanitary Committee) and Mrs Hall (Vice Chair of the Committee). In 1943, it was announced that the new hospital would be known as the Queen Elizabeth Hospital which was soon abbreviated to the QE. Building work, halted during the war, resumed and both medical and surgical facilities were in use by 1945. The QE was formally opened by Queen Elizabeth (wife of George VI) on 18th March 1948 just four months before the National Health Service began. A new Art Deco style isolation block was also opened on the site which meant that accommodation in the Isolation Hospital was increased to 120.

The Mayor, Ald Pickering, at the official opening of Greenesfield clinic.

Sheriff Hill Hospital East Ward.

The former hospital wards of the High Teams Institution were renamed Bensham General Hospital and provided a further 300 beds. Improvements were carried out here with a new 'A' block and physiotherapy unit opening in 1952. Seven years later, a new operating theatre with 45 surgical beds was opened. In 1965, it was announced that major improvements and

Queen Elizabeth Hospital, the first hospital in the country to be given this name, c. 1950.

extensions would take place at the QE – this included a new outpatients department together with the addition of 800 beds and 21 new wards.

Three years later, in 1968, thanks to the generosity of readers of the Journal newspaper, £20,000 was raised to provide a breast cancer screening service at the QE for women throughout the North East. This proved so popular that in 1971, the Director of the Unit, Stanley Wray, threatened to close the unit down if women didn't stop pestering for an appointment. The waiting list had closed two years earlier when a staggering 10,000 women were on it.

Child Health

Having a baby and bringing up children in Gateshead's slums during the 19th century could be fraught with difficulty. When a young doctor, Alfred Cox (who later became Secretary of the British Medical Association) arrived in Gateshead and decided to specialise in midwifery, he was appalled by some of the conditions he found. He was at first intrigued by the highly patterned wallpaper he discovered when he was called out to deliver a baby in a slum area but later alarmed to discover that the 'pattern' was, in fact, dead lice and he was infested with live lice within minutes of his arrival!

Conditions like this coupled with a poor fresh water supply, lack of basic sanitation and overcrowding, all contributed to a significantly high death rate in children. In 1878, this was a high 170 per 1,000 children. A slight improvement was seen by 1900 with a death rate of 167 per 1,000 but by 1921, things were certainly improving (106 per 1,000) and by 1939, the situation was a much more satisfactory 60 per 1,000. Improvements were due to a number of factors one of which included, for the first time, properly trained midwives.

Children's Hospital, Dryden Road.

However, by far the biggest cause of death was still premature birth and until further medical research was carried out there was often little hope for these babies.

The Royal Jubilee Children's Hospital opened in Gateshead on 1st October 1888 with eight beds paid for largely by legacies, local workmen and various clubs with Lord and Lady Northbourne contributing both the land on which it was built and a generous donation of £1,250. In its first full year, 75 in-patients and 754 out-patients were treated and it proved so successful that the foundation stone for a new extension, which provided two operating rooms, bath and lavatory annexes and two small wards with offices, was laid on 9th October 1907. By then, 2,369 in-patients and 16,748 out-patients had been treated. Vickers Armstrong Employees Medical Fund gave a grant of £620 in 1937 to provide a new X-ray plant.

Queen Elizabeth visited in February 1939 and was so impressed, that her daughter (the present Queen) sent a large piece of her birthday cake '*with Princess Elizabeth's best wishes to the children of the hospital*' later in the year.

New mother and baby clinics were established at Greenesfield House and also at Bensham Settlement. At these clinics it was possible to buy dried milk which was sold at discounted prices to deserving cases and in 1921, 38,881 lbs of it was distributed. The mother and baby clinics also included care and advice for expectant mothers. A report in 1938 revealed the worrying statistic that out of 32 examined, 31 expectant mothers were malnourished and not eating the recommended number of calories.

The first maternity unit opened in the Queen Elizabeth Hospital in 1944 with 34 beds, one labour suite and two labour wards. The fee was 8/- per day (reduced for the poor) with non-Gateshead residents charged 12/- per day. It was remarkable however, how many of these non-resident mothers managed to supply Gateshead addresses in order to gain the reduced fee! Children's health was often ignored but in 1909, the School Medical Service began – at first operated by doctors only – there were no nurses or other help until 1914, and in 1910, two infant welfare centres were established at Coatsworth Road and in the Masonic Hall on Jackson Street.

The laying of the foundation stone for the new extension of the Children's Hospital.

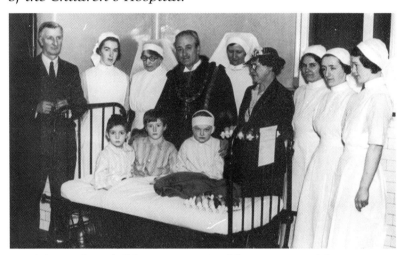

A visit to the Children's Hospital by Mayor Ald. W.J. Pickering and Mayoress, 16th April 1938.

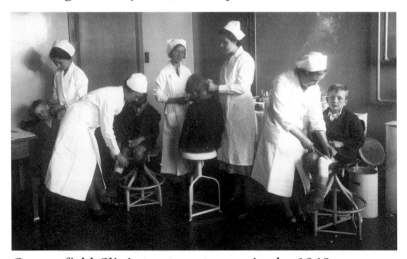

Greenesfield Clinic treatment room in the 1940s.

Dental treatment, which was offered during school inspections, was often refused due to lack of money, resulting in a generation of children growing up with poor teeth.

In 1938, ultra violet ray therapy was introduced at the new Greenesfield clinic for expectant and nursing mothers and children under five. Seventy-eight children were treated in this way for rickets. However, there was a stigma attached to unmarried mothers, illegitimate infants and homeless children who were all dealt with in the hospital wards of the High Teams Institution.

Compulsory vaccination against smallpox had been introduced in 1853 but later acts allowed parents to apply for exemption before the baby was four months old with responsibility for seeing that babies were vaccinated resting with the Board of Guardians. There were numerous cases of people being prosecuted in Gateshead for non-compliance – in 1885, two prominent local Councillors, Lancelot Tulip Penman and Thomas John Robson were each fined 2s 6d plus costs at the local Police Court for neglecting to have their children vaccinated. However, the high number of smallpox sufferers in Gateshead, compared to other towns on Tyneside, suggests that enforcement of this rule was not always carried out regularly. Many people objected to vaccinations, fearful of the scars that they would produce.

During the Second World War, there was an increase in the number of infant welfare centres in Gateshead and a very successful war time nursery opened in Holy Trinity Vicarage in 1942. This held 42 children who were all 'taught to be self-reliant' – which presumably meant potty trained! However, despite, or perhaps because of its success, high levels of infectious diseases were recorded in the nursery and so all the children who attended were hastily immunised against diphtheria.

The children's hospital in Dryden Road continued to treat cases but by 1956, many children were being sent to other hospitals with more specialised facilities which

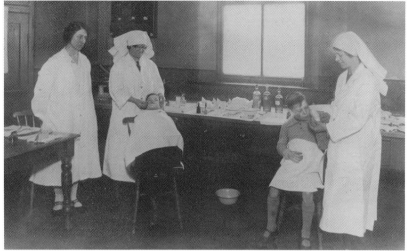

Here are three photographs showing children receiving treatment at school clinics in 1928. Below: A boy is being given an eye test. Bottom photo: A girl receives dental treatment.

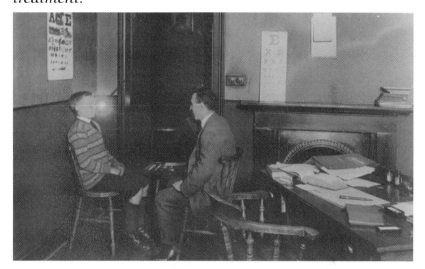

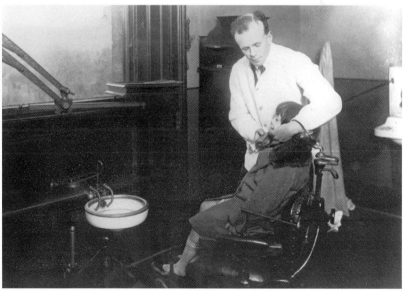

resulted in many beds lying empty. In 1959, an ante-natal outpatients opened at the Children's Hospital and the building eventually ended its days as a clinic for the deaf.

Post war, the disease feared was polio. In 1952, there was a severe outbreak of polio in Gateshead with two thirds of those affected being children under five. Most were sent to Sheriff Hill Isolation Hospital. However, the introduction of polio vaccinations in the late 1950s meant the disease was virtually eradicated within a few years.

Health Care For The Elderly

While the health situation for the rest of the population improved during the 20th century, for the elderly and infirm in Gateshead, provision largely revolved around the former workhouse hospital wards, renamed the High Teams Institution in the early 20th century. Despite improvements in 1948 when it was given a lick of paint, some new furniture and renamed Fountain View, it remained a bleak place in which to end one's life. Many of Fountain View's residents were later moved out to the new, and rather nicer, council-built old people's homes which opened in the 1950s.

For those with mental health problems, the situation was even bleaker. Two lunatic asylums, one in Sydney Grove, Bensham, the other at High Fell had catered for 'imbeciles and lunatics' in the 18th and 19th centuries. This one at Bensham (*right*) claimed in 1855 that '*It is said by many medical gentlemen to be equal to, and by some superior to Italy, for the recovery of delicate constitutions.*' High Fell was advertised for sale in 1859 providing '*An eligible opportunity for a medical gentleman who is inclined to the study and treatment of the insane.*' Despite these claims, both had closed by 1870.

The former Bensham Asylum photographed shortly before demolition in 1982.

They were replaced in 1912 by a 500-bedded mental hospital at Stannington, later called St Mary's. In 1939, a new block called Eldon House was added to this and the focus now switched to cure rather than simply care, with Gateshead regarded as a trail-blazer in this regard. However, some of Gateshead's elderly patients with mental health problems, still remained in Fountain View in what must have been a fairly miserable existence.

Fountain View in 1969 shortly before demolition.

Shortly before the building was demolished in 1969, a newspaper article described them as '*Forgotten inmates of a modern bedlam.*' It continued ' … *people who live in a building that Dickens might have known; who receive no visitors, and for whom therapy has rested in three television sets … they live out their lives in a Dickensian twilight world which the Welfare State seems to have forgotten.*'

Eventually they were moved to more suitable accommodation at Northgate Hospital at Morpeth.

Getting Help

The number of medical personnel varied throughout the years with the sharpest rise being in the number of dentists. From four in the town in 1888, this had risen to 23 within 50 years. Doctors and surgeons had a more gradual increase in numbers – from 23 in 1888 to 32 in 1939 – of which at least eight were operating in Bensham Road. Denewell Avenue in Low Fell was widely regarded as the Harley Street of Gateshead as it contained a good mix of dentists, doctors and nurses. Of course, until the inception of the National Health Service, all treatment had to be paid for and various insurance schemes were available to help offset costs.

Even so, many people delayed seeking treatment which often led to unnecessary deaths. There were alternatives to the doctors of course as there were always a variety of chemists, drugstores and herbalists to choose from (*see page 52*).

District nursing came to Gateshead in 1900 with the establishment of a nurses' home in Coatsworth Road, designed for nurses caring for the sick and poor in their own home. Walter Willson, a former Mayor of Gateshead, and founder of Walter Willson's stores (*see page 59*), had established the Gateshead Nursing Association in 1901 and his wife, who was President of the Association, paid for and opened a new extension in 1935.

Wilson's chemist's shop, Askew Road.

Nurses' Home on Coatsworth Road.

Members of St John Ambulance service practising in the grounds of J.A. Harrison's home, Saltwell Vale House, Low Fell, in 1898.

To get to hospital, an ambulance was the obvious means of transport but until the National Health Service began in 1948, this wasn't always a free service. Before this date, most were operated by the St John Ambulance Brigade. The Low Fell Division, founded by John Adolphus Harrison in 1894, was the first to be established north of Leeds.

Gateshead bought their first ambulance with money donated to the Dispensary by the executors of Councillor Gilhespy. This horse-drawn vehicle came into service in 1907 and was under the control of the Chief Constable (the police operated most of the ambulances at this time). The police got a new motor ambulance at a cost of £1,550 in April 1921 for dealing with street accidents. It held two stretchers, one of which was on wheels, heating apparatus and a tip up wash basin. In 1938, Gateshead had two ambulances specially designated for infectious diseases and in 1952, a new ambulance station was built beside the Queen Elizabeth Hospital. This cost £18,000 and could house 12 ambulances.

Public Health

Throughout the 20th century, there were major improvements in public health but these had been a long time in coming. The Cholera Commissioners enquiry of 1854 had found the town to be overcrowded, with little in the way of sanitation and most people living in dwellings not fit for habitation. Eventually the town's first sanitary inspector was appointed in 1866, followed seven years later by a (part-time) Medical Officer of Health who had a yearly salary of £25. Gradually, improvements began to be made but health reports provide ample evidence of how long it took for some of these to develop. The exasperation of the various report writers is plain to see.

In 1884, due to the high mortality rate of the town, a special enquiry was held into Gateshead's health by the Local Government Board and they found that many of the problems flagged up in the Cholera Commissioners report 30 years earlier still applied although some of the slum housing had been demolished. Removal of refuse continued to be a major problem, with middens being emptied only once every six weeks. Following the recommendations made in this report, Gateshead appointed its first full time Medical Officer of Health at £120 per year.

Gateshead was to be well served by its Medical Officers in the 20th century with Thomas Morrison Clayton, who served from 1896-1936, and James Grant his successor, who served until 1965, both providing sterling service.

By the 1930s, many of the old earth closets had been converted to flush toilets (*see page 9*) and most of the Gateshead slums had been cleared, with many of the residents moving to new council houses with their inside bathrooms and toilets. Even so, in 1944, less than half the homes in Gateshead had bathrooms. After the Second World War, there were further improvements including smoke control which was introduced into Gateshead in 1960 and by 1965, James Grant was able to record that there had been no deaths in childbirth and no real threat to people's health due to infectious diseases.

Many of the slum housing had been infested with a variety of species. In the 19th century, there was little in the way of prevention but the 20th century saw improvements. In Gateshead in 1938, 150 homes were disinfested of bedbugs – a mammoth operation which involved stripping and burning off the wallpaper, loosening skirting boards and other wood features and then applying fungicide. A further 176 tenants complained of infestation by beetles or crickets and these were also dealt with.

In 1965, the council advertised for a new replacement rat catcher – his salary was £14 13s 6d per week. He had to be *'hard working, trustworthy and smart.'* This latter requirement was in case he had to be speedily sent to the Town Hall to deal with invading rodents!

By the end of the 20th century the problems which had originally caused so much ill health had disappeared. But yesterday's

deprivation has been replaced by today's excess, and obesity and dietary health are current health concerns. When the photograph above was taken at the High Teams Institution in 1927, both the Mayor, Alderman Wardill and Alderman Clough to the right are holding cigarettes – then often considered healthy for those with chest conditions. A photograph like this would not be published today!

Chapter Seven
Sunday Best

Until 1825, people really had no choice over which church to attend in Gateshead – it was St Mary's Church, sitting high above the Quayside or nothing. But the 19th and early 20th centuries were to see a positive explosion in the number of opportunities made available for people to worship, with churches, chapels and missions springing up in seemingly unlimited numbers throughout Gateshead. Roman Catholics, Methodists, Presbyterians, Congregationalists, and Baptists all had their own churches by 1900. Some were grand, some were small; some were 'high', some were 'low'; some were for the rich who came in their carriages, and others were attended by the working classes; but all provided a focal point for people to go to on Sundays. This was also an opportunity to get dressed up, even if, for the poor, this often revolved around getting the 'Sunday best' out of the pawnshop on Saturday evening and returning them on Monday morning.

And then there were all the spin-offs from Church to join – Sunday schools, choirs, girls' and boys' brigades, women's and men's fellowships – these were just a few of the various activities associated with church or chapel going. Going to church was often about much more than religion on its own and, particularly in the 19th century, it provided a stabilising influence at a time of great industrial and consequent social change.

But to begin with, there was only one church to attend. This was St Mary's, Gateshead's 'mother church', in existence from the 12th century until 1979 when a disastrous fire (compounded by a further fire in 1983) ended the building's use as a place of worship. St Mary's had a series of excellent ministers. The 19th century reforming Edward Prest did away with pew rents, began a service collection and encouraged a revival in psalm and hymn singing. His successor, William Moore Ede, rector from 1881, quite aside from his praiseworthy church work, brought the penny-dinner system to hundreds of Gateshead school children; and Canon Stephenson, St Mary's longest serving Rector almost had to be forcibly retired after an incumbency of over 40 years in 1956.

Edward Prest, as well as reviving St Mary's congregation with a dose of evangelical zeal, deserves an extra mention as he was responsible for the creation of several new parishes in Gateshead – necessary as Gateshead's population steadily expanded to areas outside the town centre. In stark contrast, Canon Stephenson could only watch in dismay in the 1930s as the effects of Gateshead's slum clearance programme virtually cleared his parish of resident parishioners.

The commemorative service for the death of George V on 28th January 1936. The mace bearer leads the Town Clerk William Porter and the Mayor, James White into St Mary's Church.

Despite the creation of these other churches and other parishes, it was usually St Mary's which remained the venue for major services in Gateshead. Royal commemorative services such as those for the death of Queen Victoria, and the Coronation of Queen Elizabeth II were all held here. It was also the scene of many Civic services, especially Mayor's Sunday, although as the 19th century progressed into the 20th century, increasingly buildings belonging to other denominations were used. In 1910, the new Mayor, pawnbroker William John Costelloe caused a storm of protest when he announced he wished his mayoral service to take place at St Joseph's RC Church – to which, incidentally, he had provided a magnificent marble altar and new marble communion rails three years previously. He got his wish but not without a struggle.

The first new Anglican Church to be built in Gateshead after St Mary's (a period of about 700 years), was St John's at Sheriff Hill – still today, due to its elevated position and tall spire, a local landmark. The church was created as part of the 1809 enclosure of Gateshead Fell which created this new parish and it opened in 1825. An 1883 restoration saw extra pews fitted and an organ loft built on the north side. The church has seen some disasters – in October 1862 a severe gale damaged the spire which meant that the top 37 feet had to be rebuilt and it very nearly burnt down in 1928 when some pews caught fire.

The famous American singer Paul Robeson gave a free public concert here on 7th May 1949 and performed many of his best known songs including 'Old Man River' and 'Swing low, sweet chariot' to packed crowds both inside and outside the church.

Gateshead's third church was Holy Trinity – the name given to the John Dobson restoration of the former St Edmund's Chapel on Gateshead High Street (not to be confused with St Edmund's chapel on Old Durham Road, dedicated to

Holy Trinity with the Ellison Schools to the left, c. 1893.

a different St Edmund). This was a building, which, like St Mary's, had a long history. Re-founded as the Hospital of Saint Edmund Bishop & Confessor in 1248, it belonged to the nuns of St Bartholomew's Nunnery in Newcastle from 1480 until the dissolution of the monasteries led to its demise in 1540. It then fell into a state of disrepair until Cuthbert Ellison (Gateshead's Lord of the Manor) paid for its restoration in 1837 as a chapel of ease to St Mary's. By the 1880s it was seen as too small as it could only seat 200 on what were described as uncomfortable seats and it was threatened with demolition. The Society of Antiquaries of Newcastle were alarmed at this threat to the church, and *sent a deputation to argue for preservation*. It was only their intervention which saved the Church from almost certain destruction. Lord Northbourne, a great benefactor to many churches in Gateshead (including the Church of the Venerable Bede, and St Paul's at Low Teams) gave £4,000 towards enlarging it. The existing church became the south aisle of the new larger Holy Trinity which was designed by Stephen Piper and it opened in 1893. In 1918, parishioners 'saw the light' literally when electric lights were installed.

St Cuthbert's became Gateshead's fourth Anglican Church when it was built by John Dobson

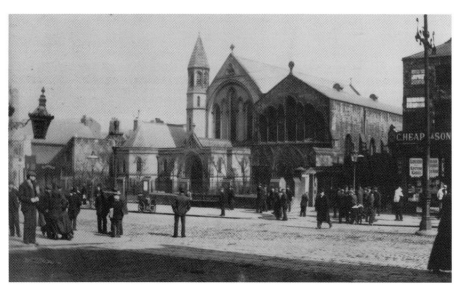

Holy Trinity with its extension. The building to the right is the flour premises of C. Heap & Sons.

as a chapel of ease to St Mary's in 1848. It was later given its own parish in 1865. The rather appropriately named Reverend Parrish caused a storm of controversy over, of all things, altar candles, during the First World War. Parrish had come from Holy Trinity, regarded as 'high church' while St Cuthbert's was 'low church'. He wanted candles on the altar – the congregation didn't. Eventually a compromise was reached and the vicar was allowed just one candle but only for the duration of the war.

By the time St Cuthbert's was built, Methodism was becoming a rising force in Gateshead and to combat this, the number of Church of England churches rose rapidly as the 19th century progressed. In 1846 there were only four Anglican churches, but this number had doubled by 1889. These included St Helen's at Low Fell, the money for which was provided by Edward Joicey, the coal owner of neighbouring Whinney House, Low Fell, who earned the gratitude of his parishioners as they no longer had to face the long uphill trek to St John's.

By 1909, there were 13 Anglican churches in Gateshead and a number of mission rooms in some of the more heavily populated areas of town. Gateshead's grandest Anglican church opened in 1903. Popularly titled 'Bensham's Cathedral', St Chad's was an architecturally beautiful building with a magnificent octagonal clock tower and an Arts and Crafts interior. This church was the gift of Miss Emily Matilda Easton whose family had owned the Nest Colliery in Felling. Had it not been for Miss Easton, the 'large industrial population' which it was claimed the church would serve, might not have received nearly such a grand building.

The rather plain interior of St Cuthbert's photographed in 1893.

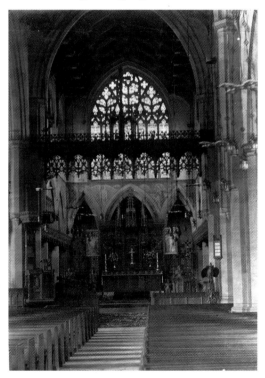

St Chad's magnificent exterior c. 1930 and its Arts and Crafts interior (right).

Some churches started their lives as tin churches. These were obtained in kit form and formed a temporary structure while a 'proper' building was being planned. Examples of these included St George's on Durham Road, St Paul's at Low Teams, St Andrew's on Westfield Terrace and the Presbyterian Church on Dryden Road. Tin churches could create interesting sound effects due to weather conditions as, for example, the sound of 'gun shots' which could unnerve the congregation but were simply the metal sheeting expanding during hot weather!

But, while the Church of England was busily constructing new churches and creating extra parishes, the various branches of Methodism were busy too.

John Wesley, the founder of Methodism, had made frequent well documented visits to Gateshead in the 18th century, finding many of the town's inhabitants in need of religion. In 1743 he resolved to visit *'a little village called Chowden (Chowdene) which they told me consisted of colliers only. I resolved to preach there as soon as possible, for these are sinners and need repentance.'*

He was to preach here and at Low Fell many times and used a small house (now demolished) on Church Road which became the first Methodist preaching house in County Durham. The congregation frequently overspilled the cramped conditions and Wesley often had to preach standing on a huge stone outside the house.

The novelist and poet Rudyard Kipling also had a connection to Methodism in Gateshead as his grandfather, the Reverend Joseph Kipling, was a Methodist Minister in Gateshead between 1850-52 and Kipling's maternal grandfather, the Rev G.B. Macdonald preached the sermon at the evening service when High West Street Methodist Church opened.

Methodism split into three principal strands – the Wesleyans, the Primitive Methodists and the New Connexion. They all had differing styles of worship and consequently tended to build different buildings – those of the Wesleyan Methodists being much more ornate and appealing to the more affluent members of society than those of the Primitive Methodists and New Connexion whose buildings tended to be smaller and plainer.

One of the most ornate of these buildings in Gateshead was the Wesleyan Methodist Church situated on Bensham Road. With its colonnaded classical exterior, this was far grander in appearance than was its 'opposition' – St Cuthbert's – on the opposite side of Cuthbert Street. This church, which cost about £3,000 and opened in 1873, was entirely paid for by Samuel Southern and his sister-in-law Miss Brown. Samuel, his wife and sister-in-law were great benefactors to many Methodist churches and chapels in the area and also provided money for the Wesleyan Memorial Church on Durham Road, Low Fell.

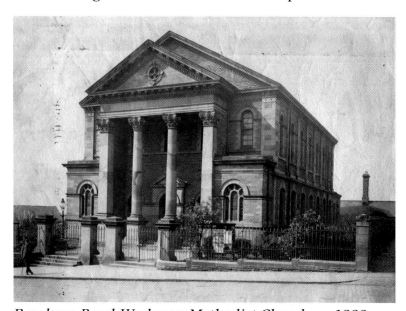

Bensham Road Wesleyan Methodist Church, c. 1900.

Another imposing Wesleyan Methodist building was the High West Street Chapel (*right, c. 1903*) which opened on 12th December 1861. Known as 'the mother church of Gateshead Methodism', this was situated at the junction of High West Street and Belle Vue Terrace. In 1933, this building was transformed into a modern Central Hall (Mission Hall) at a cost of £6,000.

Neither of these buildings are with us today but two which remain are St Mark's at Shipcote and the Wesley Memorial Church in Low Fell. St Mark's

was originally simply known as Shipcote Methodist Church and was built in 1906 with stone from Beacon Lough quarry by Alexander Pringle who later built the Cenotaph and the Central Library in Shipcote. The foundation stone for the Wesley Methodist Chapel was laid on 3rd November 1881 and provided a suitable location for the well-heeled Low Fell Methodists to worship. This location however had been hard to find as a number of other sites had been proposed but found unsuitable. It was not until building had stalled following completion of a half crescent of houses that the remainder of the plot was up for sale and the Wesleyans took their chance. The huge stone on which Wesley had stood to preach at the Church Road Meeting House was engraved and mounted into the west wall of the church hall built in 1885.

John Wesley was not the only preacher of note who came to Gateshead. When William Booth arrived in Gateshead as a New Connexion Minister in 1858, he soon revitalised the Bethesda Chapel and from congregations of less than 200, within months crowds were coming to hear him preach and attendances were reaching 2,000. When William's wife, Catherine, *'felt the spirit of the Lord'* come upon her at Pentecost in 1860, and also began to preach, she was seen as something of a novelty and received invitations to preach at various locations. At her first sermon, the chapel was *'crowded to the doors, and people sat on the very window-sills.'* She turned out to be just as good a preacher as was her husband and so many converts to the New Connexion were made here that the local ironworkers christened the building 'the converting shop'.

Another branch of Methodism was Primitive Methodism which certainly didn't get off to a good start in Gateshead. 'The Prims' were too poor to pay the rent on their first preaching room in Garden Street in 1822 and then used a variety of rooms including one in the Brandy Vaults public house from which they were expelled for making too much noise! In 1838 they managed to buy premises in Mulgrave Terrace but two years later, their treasurer absconded with the chapel funds and the building was sold to the Presbyterians.

Eventually however, they became more successful and by 1900, had chapels throughout Gateshead. Their buildings, like those of the New Connexion, tended to be simple in style and were designed to appeal to the working classes. They were often found in the mining districts of town and examples include the little Providence Chapel which opened at Sheriff Hill in 1864; Chowdene Primitive Methodist Chapel which opened in 1880; and the Primitive Methodist Chapel on Durham Road which replaced a mission in Worcester Street.

Sunday School outside the Providence Chapel, Sheriff Hill, 1907.

The last Primitive Methodist Chapel to be built in Gateshead was on Whitehall Road. The foundation stone was laid on 9th May 1925 but in 1932, the Wesleyans and the Primitive Methodists resolved their doctrinal differences and formed the Methodist Church.

Whilst the Church of England and the various sects of Methodism were busily erecting buildings, the Roman Catholics in Gateshead had much fewer premises. Their first services were held in a makeshift chapel in the top storey of a warehouse in Hillgate which was later destroyed in the Great Fire of 1854 and they then used rooms in the Queen's Head on Bottle Bank. However, due to the generosity of Gateshead's Irish workforce who provided funds out of their small earnings to get themselves a place of

Laying of the foundation stone at Durham Road Primitive Methodist Chapel, 1893.

worship, St Joseph's Roman Catholic Church opened at the corner of Walker Terrace and High West Street in 1859. Planned to be called Our Lady and St Wilfrid's, the name was changed prior to the opening as it was thought confusion might be caused with the recently built St Mary's in Newcastle (designed by the same architect, Archibald Dunn). The church, however, was not built as planned, as can be seen in this architect's drawing (right). Probably, once the church was opened, the bell tower was thought of as mere ornamentation and not worth subscribing to.

This shows St Joseph's as a more ornate building with a bell tower.

It would be 50 years before another Roman Catholic Church opened. This was Our Lady and St Wilfrid, converted from a former school in 1904 to serve the population living in the Tyneside flats off Sunderland Road. This was replaced in 1955.

As the Bensham and Saltwell districts grew in size, there were demands by the parishioners for their own Roman Catholic Church to replace the school chapel which they had been using since 1909. Finally on 14th April 1936, their wish was granted when Corpus Christi

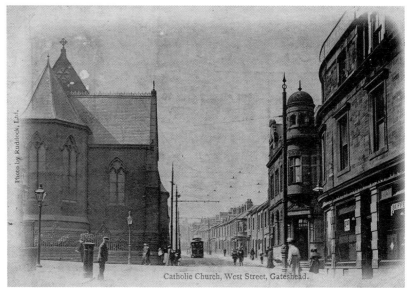

This shows St Joseph's Church with Walker Terrace and the Old Mill public house at the right of the photograph.

opened. This cost £13,000 and could seat 500. A contemporary newspaper described this rather modest church as *'Designed and built by Tynesiders'.*

Further churches were built at Low Fell (St Peter's) and the Teams area (Holy Rosary). When St Peter's parish was formed in 1929, and before premises were built, Sunday mass was held above the Meadow Dairy's store on Durham Road with parishioners asked to bring their own chairs to sit on!

But as well as Church of England, Methodists and Roman Catholics, there were other sects in Gateshead. The Gateshead Presbyterian and Congregational churches had their origins in Newcastle and had it not been for some mean minded parishioners, Presbyterianism might not have appeared in Gateshead quite as early as it did. When an 18th century Presbyterian Minister in Newcastle, Alan Cornforth, married a widow with 12 children, his congregation *'rebelled against so large a burden being placed upon*

Interior of Corpus Christi in the 1930s.

their shoulders.' He came to Gateshead and opened a building in Mirk Lane on New Year's Day 1786, using old pews from other Newcastle churches. Mr Cornforth's salary was so low that in one year he received out of the funds *'a suit of clothes, he being much in want.'*

In 1845, a former Congregational building in Ellison Street West was bought. Once the congregation began to expand, thanks largely to its successful minister, John Jeffrey, there began to be frequent complaints about the building's condition. A new site on Windmill Hills was purchased and Park Terrace Presbyterian Church opened on 1st January 1889 with a congregation almost wholly working class. By 1936, there were four Presbyterian churches in town – Park Terrace (the mother church); Durham Road; Brighton Road and Low Fell. The Durham Road church was situated at the junction with Bewick Road – a site which, because of the proximity of two other churches, the United Methodist Church and the Baptist Church, became known locally as 'Amen Corner'.

Congregationalists appeared in Gateshead in 1836 when the rope-making Haggie brothers provided the site mentioned above in Ellison Street West. It wasn't a success and neither was another building which they took over in Park Lane. Eventually, after having used the Town Hall for a short time, they bought a new site on Bensham Road and the foundation stone for a new church was laid in 1872. The Trustees were all upper class – solicitors, ship owners and the like but the congregation was largely working class.

The Baptists had their first church in 1877 at the corner of Gladstone terrace with Durham Road (*see photo below*).

'Amen Corner' with the Baptist Church on the left, the Presbyterian Church with the spire next to it, and the United Methodist Free Church on the right.

One of the more unusual churches in Gateshead was the Unity Church on Coatsworth Road, set apart by its trust which stated that it was *'for the worship of God by the congregation who may from time to time assemble.'*

One humble little building, the Vine Street Mission, deserves a special mention. This was founded by Sister Winifred Laver (*see also page 62*) in 1915 when she came to Gateshead and discovered the dreadful poverty that many families were experiencing. A saint in a modern world, Sister Winifred worked tirelessly, supplying food for those too poor to afford it. She thought nothing of taking hundreds of children to the seaside for summer outings and provided Christmas parties for them.

But no matter what the style of architecture or the size of the premises, all churches and chapels had music in some forms. Sometimes this took the form of a large organ as was the case with St George's Church on Durham Road where a magnificent 'Father' Willis organ was installed in 1906. Often, however, smaller organs, harmoniums or pianos were used (*see photograph on page 4*).

Church and chapel choirs were a strong feature of church life – as can be seen in this photograph of St Cuthbert's choir, taken outside Gateshead rectory on Bensham Road in the early years of the 20th century, some of these choirs were substantial in size.

At St Mary's Church, Canon Stephenson began special Ascension Day services when the choir boys had to climb up the stairs and sing on the roof – this must have been a challenge for any who had no head for heights!

Most churches and chapels had Sunday Schools. The photograph right shows the Sunday School teachers at St Columba's Church in 1922. For a comparatively modest church, there are a surprising large number of people. There were also numerous social groups attached to churches. In 1949, Brighton Avenue Presbyterian Church alone had the following: Young Men's Literary Institute, Sunday

school, League of Young Worshippers, Girls' Life Brigade, Boys' Brigade, Life Boys, Fellowship of Youth, Women's Own, Women's Missionary Association, a Badminton Club and a drama group 'The Brighton Avenue Players'.

If the 19th century was a time of church expansion, from the mid 20th century it was one of contraction. There were various reasons for this. Some were due to previously separate sects (Methodism was a good example of this) joining together which made many churches superfluous. Others were closed due to fires such as St Mary's (although this had already been scheduled for closure) and the Church of the Holy Rosary. St Edmund's Church on Old Durham Road closed after storms damaged its roof which then proved too costly to repair. Others were simply in the way of new developments – the Methodist Central Hall was flattened to build the Civic Centre and the Durham Road Presbyterian Church building was demolished with the Five Bridges Hotel (later The Swallow) built on the site. But also, the ever decreasing numbers of people attending churches and chapels had a significant impact on many of the 19th and early 20th century church buildings. Their architecture was not always well regarded either – a Council handbook in 1969 stated that '*The churches of the nineteenth century are ... of no great historical interest.*'

Gale damage at St Edmund's in 1969. The church was demolished two years later.

Fortunately one survivor proved to be St Edmund's on the High Street. Once merely the south aisle of Holy Trinity, this came into its own again following Holy Trinity's closure and conversion into a community centre. Reverting back to its original name, the building, as well as being a fully functioning church, now also houses an art space. St Mary's Church also has a new use as a heritage centre.

Other buildings, now demolished, also had interesting later uses. One of these was St Hilda's Mission Church which opened in 1903. It later became Bensham Roller Skating Rink before being demolished in the early 1970s, while Belle Vue Methodist Chapel was converted to YMCA premises, for which £20,000 was contributed by Sir Arthur Sutherland, ship owner and philanthropist. Booth's Bethesda Chapel became Howe Brothers, printers, while Kelly Brothers, another printing firm, used the Congregational Church building in Ellison Street West.

Today, although there are less churches, and far fewer churchgoers going to them, present churchgoers tend not to have to get their 'Sunday best' out of the pawnbrokers!

Members of the Wesleyan Methodist Church, Bensham Road, all dressed up ready for their Good Friday outing on 28th March 1902.

Chapter Eight
In Our Spare Time

Before the Factory Acts in the late 19th century created the new concept of half days and days off for workers, most people didn't have much leisure time. But when they got it, what did they do with it?

For many people in Gateshead, this all revolved around cost and availability. For example, Saltwell Park, a free attraction, was seen when it opened in 1876 as 'in the country' and, until 1901, when the electric trams began operating a service to it, couldn't be reached by public transport. This put it beyond the reach of many of the poor in the slums of the High Street and the Quayside who faced a long trudge through the town and then through fields to reach this oasis of splendour. They did however, have a rather less splendid alternative in the shape of Windmill Hills – the town's first public park, although this was really an area of greenery rather than a traditional park landscape.

For those who were prepared to make the journey to Saltwell Park, beautiful floral displays, refreshment pavilions, a selection of animals and birds, a boating lake and bowling greens were just some of the early attractions on offer and these were all added to during the 20th century. Regular Sunday afternoon band concerts were also held, even if for a few years, these were held on the island in the lake which meant that when the wind blew in the wrong direction no one could hear them! The lake also became the scene where, on Sunday mornings, members of the Model Boat Club would gather to sail their boats – a tradition which has continued to this day.

In 1933, Saltwell Towers was converted into Gateshead's Local and Industrial Museum which proved a great attraction to young and old, particularly in its early years when it was common to have to join a lengthy queue for admission. However, in 1969, the Towers finally succumbed to the dry rot which had threatened it for most of its existence, with the result that it was hastily closed and the exhibits dispersed.

Parks were not only seen as beneficial to health but were free. Other free attractions in Gateshead were the public libraries and the Shipley Gallery.

Small private libraries had existed in Gateshead from the 18th century but the public library movement was a Victorian development. The 1851 Public Libraries Act had allowed Councils to levy an extra penny on the rates for

The bandstand on the island.

'Are you being served?' The Grahamsley Street shop front in Saltwell Park Museum, 18th April 1952.

the provision of a library service, something which Gateshead councillors, keen to keep their seats, were unwilling to do. However, once Newcastle decided to adopt the Act, there was pressure on Gateshead to do the same and in 1880 a vote was held at the Town Hall to determine whether the library rate should be levied. The result was so close that a Burgess vote was demanded, which resulted in a narrow majority vote of 32 in favour. Over four times that number applied for the post of librarian when this was first advertised!

Gateshead's first public library opened in 1884 on Swinburne Street but almost from the start was considered too small. New premises were already being discussed before the First World War but costs rocketed and a much smaller library than was originally planned opened on Prince Consort Road in 1926. This was in the Shipcote area of town – an area regarded as a much more desirable neighbourhood than the town centre, from which to borrow books. Now, for the first time, Gateshead readers could go directly to the shelves to choose their books instead of the previous lengthy process of selecting books from a catalogue then having to check an indicator board to see if they were 'in' or 'out'.

The new library was hugely popular (during the Second World War, the library was issuing a staggering average of 2,500 books per day) and it wasn't long before there were demands for branch libraries in other parts of town. Sunderland Road Library opened in September 1934 by the Mayor, Timothy Armstrong. This was a decidedly home grown building as it was designed by Fred Pattinson, the Borough Surveyor and built by C.P. Smith & Sons of Wrekenton. Another branch library opened at Redheugh on 1st June 1939. Further new purpose built libraries opened in Wrekenton, Lobley Hill and Low Fell after the war. At all libraries, story times were a regular feature and as the photograph below shows, were attended by many enthusiastic children.

Children selecting their books in the junior section of Gateshead Central Library in 1960.

But books weren't the only things to read in libraries. Newspapers were also heavily used, both by the unemployed who would turn up at the library at opening time to scour the papers for job advertisements, and those wanting to read the latest current affairs and sports news. Those hoping to find any horse racing tips however, would have been disappointed as, for many years, Gateshead Libraries obliterated anything connected with betting, seeing it as their duty to protect the poor from potentially gambling their money away.

Although for a few years Gateshead had a School of Art (housed upstairs in the old Swinburne Street Library), they never had an art gallery until the Shipley Gallery opened on Thursday, 29th November 1917, having

Central Library story time with Miss O. Hill in the 1930s.

had special permission to be completed during the First World War. The gallery was the result of a bequest by Joseph Aynsley Davidson Shipley – resident of Saltwell Towers and a Newcastle solicitor – who died in 1909. Shipley was a lifelong, although somewhat undiscriminating, collector of paintings and left 2,500 of them in his will, together with £30,000 which was intended to be given to Newcastle for the extension or building of a new art gallery. Newcastle called in experts to value the paintings and they decided that many were copies or simply fakes. Eventually, Newcastle turned down the bequest which was then offered to Gateshead. Gateshead agreed to accept it and land was identified for a gallery at Shipcote alongside Gateshead Secondary School. Gateshead kept the 371 paintings believed to be originals and added a further 130 paintings – the rest were sold at auction achieving an average price of £4 each. Matthew Young (*see photo on page 28*), who had previously been Joseph Shipley's office boy, was appointed as the first curator of the gallery, which was built to the latest concepts in gallery planning with large roof lights allowing maximum light into the four gallery spaces.

Along with its neighbour, the Central Library, the art gallery proved a popular leisure attraction although not always for the purpose intended as the photograph right of children, happily enjoying a puppet show in the gallery, shows. Many however, are more interested in the photographer!

Sport, of course, had always been a popular leisure time pursuit – not only to take part in but also to watch and support. Hoppings on Windmill Hills in the early years of the 19th century advertised a wide variety of races such as running for a hat, running for a cheese (this was for men tied up in sacks!) and wrestling for tobacco. One popular early sport which was centred around the public house was cock fighting although this was more common in the 18th than the 19th century.

But the main spectator sport of the 19th century was rowing, which from 1821 for the next 50 years attracted huge crowds who would stand packed along the quayside, cheerfully waving on their favourites as they took on other rowers, or teams of rowers, on the Tyne. This was a sport on which huge sums of money could be bet and the Tyne rowers and their boats, which developed into real racing boats, became famous. The three best rowers were Harry Clasper, Robert 'Honest Bob' Chambers and, the greatest of them all, James Renforth (*left*). Sadly all three died within a few years of each other and their deaths, coupled with the Tyne Commissioners action in dredging the river (which included removing the small islands which formed part of the course), resulted in a decline in this sport from the mid 1870s onwards.

Other sports in the 19th century included bowls, boxing and cycling. The Gateshead Bowling Green Club, with their grounds on Prince Consort Road, was first established in 1865, initially as a quoits club. Quoits was a popular 18th and 19th century sport but had declined in popularity by the 1930s. Bowling however, has continued with a number of greens in Gateshead. Saltwell Park had its first bowling green (unusual as it was octagonal in shape) in 1878 and by the outbreak of the Second World War, five more greens had been added, all of which were very popular. Bowls was described by a visitor to the park

James Renforth in a studio photograph.

in 1910 as '… *a fine healthy game suitable for young, old and middle aged.*' For many years there was an annual bowling tournament which was usually opened by the Mayor of Gateshead. Another green, the Lyndhurst Bowling Green, opened at Low Fell in 1906. This, like Saltwell Park, also contained tennis courts.

Tennis developed as a popular sport from the 1880s onwards but ladies found that they were hampered by their long skirts. Shorter skirts were developed – however, the first two young ladies spotted wearing these in Saltwell Park in 1919 were reported to the Park Superintendent for indecency!

Boxing was a dangerous sport and was frowned on until the adoption of the Queensberry Rules though this still did not prevent serious accidents in the ring. Boxing in Gateshead took place in a number of venues – one of the main ones being the Standard Theatre in Sunderland Road. This was where you could sometimes see Will Curley (1876-1937) the featherweight boxer who was one of the first glove champions at the turn of the 20th century. After his retirement he became licensee of the Phoenix Inn on the High Street – now simply called Curley's Bar.

There was a boom in cycling once the safety bicycle was developed in the 1880s although cycling here lost popularity after the early 1900s. Cycle races were organised at the North Durham cricket and rugby football ground which had a cement lined and cambered cycle track. One of the first clubs was the Tynevale Amateur Cycling Club which was captained by George Brown (*see page 50*). At first, this was seen as something of a male pursuit but soon ladies began to take it up. One of these was Mary Spence Watson of Bensham Grove, who wrote in her

The octagonal bowling green in use in 1907.

The Mayor, Councillor John Maccoy, opens the annual bowls tournament in 1923.

The Tynevale Amateur Cycling Club in 1895.

'Reminiscences': '*In the summer on Saturdays as we grew older, parties of us went cycling, getting tea out at a village Inn. My sister Evelyn was one of the first lady cyclists in these parts, and it was not at all approved by the general public, who made insulting remarks. Bertha and I were the first to bicycle in 'rational dress', very different to the shorts girls wear now-a-days. We were rather proud of it, but there was a good deal of dislike of it … tho' our parents were very tolerant.'* Rational dress was a looser style of dress than the tight fitting and corseted fashion styles of the 19th and early 20th centuries.

If rowing was the spectator sport of the 19th century, then football was the spectator sport of the 20th century. This was a sport which many could enjoy and many schools and even churches had their own teams. Charity matches were often held – the photograph right shows the National Union of Railwaymen's (NUR) annual 'orphan fund effort' football match which took place on 15th April 1938 at Gateshead Secondary School with Gateshead NUR playing against Newcastle NUR.

Gateshead's first 'proper' team was the Gateshead North Eastern Railway Football Club who were established in 1889. Gateshead Town however, was their earliest prominent club and they joined the Northern Football Alliance in 1905, turning professional in 1911. Early grounds were located at the Shuttles in the Teams and Old Fold Park. However, this club folded in 1924 and it was not until South Shields football club were in financial trouble that Gateshead had a football team again.

South Shields AFC needed to relocate from their Horsley Hill ground in South Shields. Gateshead offered them a home and so they changed their name to Gateshead AFC. Various sites for a new ground were considered but eventually a worked out clay pit in the Teams area was chosen and levelled by filling with refuse. This was Redheugh Park and the first game was played on 30th August 1930 when a crowd of over 15,000 spectators cheered Gateshead on to beat Doncaster Rovers 2-1. At first, gates were high but then spectator numbers dropped. However, in 1938 the club signed the ex-Newcastle United star footballer, Hughie Gallagher, for £500.

Hughie was then nearing the end of his career but when he scored five goals in his first match for the team, hopes were high for renewed success. However, the Second World War stopped any hopes of a resurgence (it also effectively ended Gallagher's professional playing career) and by the beginning of the 1950s attendances had slumped. However, amazingly in 1953, a run of good games led them to be drawn against Bolton Wanderers in the sixth round of the FA Cup. Football fever then struck Gateshead.

A cartoon from the Sunday Sun, 18th September 1938, celebrating Gallagher's five goals against Rotherham.

The Rush for Tickets

On 25th February 1953, the sixth round tickets went on sale at the Town Hall. An orderly queue had begun to form from 11 pm the previous night. Women in the queue spent their time knitting and drinking flasks of tea. At 4 pm, the tickets went on sale – by this time a staggering 11,000 people were waiting. Police were on hand to keep order but at this stage everyone was good natured and waiting patiently. By 5.45 pm, only 100 tickets were left, but nearly 10,000 people were still in the queue. Many men, now finished work, had taken their wives places in the queue but became impatient with the apparently slow sale of the tickets and began to try to rush the queue.

Seventy policemen battled for 20 minutes to restore order. An eight foot high stone pillar, at the corner of Nelson Street alongside the Town Hall, was pushed over and struck Mrs Edna Parkinson of Saltwell Street who had been waiting for tickets as a surprise for her husband. She was taken to hospital with a broken leg but later had to have her foot amputated. Once order was restored, the remaining tickets were withdrawn from sale and added to those allocated for factories and works in the town. Mrs Parkinson, by way of compensation, did, however, receive two free tickets to the match.

In the end, a goal by Nat Lofthouse following a disputed hand-ball, led to Gateshead being knocked out of the Cup. A crowd of 17,692 watched the match at Redheugh Park.

Regular team members included brothers Tom and Jack Callender, who established a record for the most appearances by two brothers at one club. In the photograph below, both brothers are shown.

Right: Gateshead AFC preparing for their Cup match against Liverpool at Redheugh Park on 9th January 1953. From left to right: Jack Callender, Bobby Grey, Tom Callender, Billy March. The player jumping is Albert Stubbins, then a player with Liverpool, but as the former Newcastle forward lived in Gateshead, was allowed to train at Redheugh Park.

During 1958-59 Gateshead played in the fourth division but had a bad season and eventually were voted out of the football league. Finally, after various problems and changes of name, the club re-formed as Gateshead FC in 1977. Nicknamed 'The Heed', they now play their games at Gateshead International Stadium. Redheugh Park is no more as it was bulldozed in 1972 and became part of the site of the Gateshead Garden Festival in 1990.

Greyhound racing appealed to many and to try and increase gate money, a dog track was added to Redheugh Park in 1937. This was successful and did boost the income for a time – however, the inclusion of the track meant that the stadium capacity was limited and the size of the playing area was reduced.

Athletics, or 'pedestrianism' to use its Victorian name, had always been a popular spectator sport and there was a running track near Friar's Goose in East Gateshead. Gateshead had two successful 19th century runners in the shape of James Rowan and James White who were contemporaries of each other. James Rowan, 'The Little Black', was world champion over 10 miles at the age of 19 and became a Victorian superstar who could draw crowds of 25,000 spectators. Sadly, fame and fortune went to his head and he died at the age of 27, buried in an unmarked pauper's grave in Gateshead East Cemetery. James White, 'The Gateshead Clipper', was equally successful and set a British record in 1863 when he ran six miles in 29 minutes and 50 seconds – a record which was unbeaten for the next 70 years. Unlike Rowan however, he did not succumb to fame and went on to become a successful athletics trainer in London.

Gradually more and more people wanted to take part in running, something which provided the impetus for the formation of Gateshead Harriers. The club was originally formed as Gateshead St Mary's Harriers (for men only) in 1904 with one of their earliest races being the annual Nowell Challenge Cup which involved a seven mile run around the Chowdene area. Activities ceased during the First World War but it re-formed, this time as Gateshead Harriers and Athletics Club and added a walking and cycling section. Women were allowed to join the club in 1951. Much later, in the 1960s, Brendan Foster was a member of the boys' team and was coached by a former walking champion and longstanding member of the club, Stan Long (who went on to be the British team coach for long distance running at the Montreal Olympics in 1976).

Gateshead International Stadium was opened as Gateshead Youth Stadium, by the former international athlete Jim Peters, on 27th August 1955. The stadium was built on the site of a former chemical works spoil heap and the idea for its creation seems to have come from the then Mayor of Gateshead, J.T. Etherington, as an activity to combat youth crime. The original facilities were fairly basic – little more than an asphalt cycling track and a cinder running track with a seating area and floodlights added later. When Brendan Foster discovered that a new synthetic running track was being planned for the stadium, he made a promise that if this was created, he would not only run at the stadium but break the world record in the process. This became the impetus behind the first 'Gateshead Games' held in 1974 which effectively put the stadium on the athletics map with Foster breaking the 3,000 metre record on 3rd August 1974 and provided it with its new name of Gateshead International Stadium. Further improvements have continued into the 21st century.

'Fun runs' first appeared in Gateshead in 1977, designed for people who did not consider themselves as serious runners. The first race was a two mile road run around the exterior of the Stadium and about 600 people turned up to take part. Today, fun runs are a regular activity.

Gateshead's first swimming baths were opened in Mulgrave Terrace in 1891 and contained one swimming pool plus 25 slipper baths. As capacity was limited, it was planned to open new baths at Shipcote and the foundation stone was laid by Ald. McCretton on 24th July 1939. The baths had been planned well before this and Shipcote farm had been demolished in 1931 to make way for them but lack of

A swimming lesson at Mulgrave Terrace baths, c. 1930. Many of these costumes would have been knitted in wool– when wet, they could stretch to fairly lengthy proportions!

money caused delays. In his speech, the Mayor said the baths would be '*A monument to the town of physical fitness*'. The Second World War further delayed construction but nevertheless, the baths opened during the war in 1942.

Other than sport and cultural attractions, what else could you do in your spare time? If you didn't mind getting up early, the 19th century Gateshead Early Rising Association might have been an option. One of its founder members was the Liberal politician Robert Spence Watson of Bensham Grove, while other members (there were only 16) included professional men of Gateshead such as the antiquarian and fellow Quaker, Robert Coltman Clephan. Rules were strict – members met each morning during the summer months at Ravensworth Villa (off Bensham Road) at 6.15 am and walked for a distance of about five miles before breakfast. Fines were incurred if members did not attend or were late!

Annual outings were always something to look forward to and most churches, clubs and public houses organised these treats. Trips organised by public houses were often 'men only' jaunts. Works outings were common too. The photograph below shows some of Clarke Chapman's workforce ready for their charabanc outing in about 1914. And sometimes whole streets would organise outings. (*See bottom photograph rear cover*).

For many years, the Mayor of Gateshead took his councillors and high ranking officials on a picnic. In the photograph below taken at Greta Bridge, near Barnard Castle, the Mayor, Councillor Timothy Armstrong, is seated centre wearing a hat, with his wife on his left. Though taken on 25th July 1934, there are no concessions either to informality or to the summer weather! The group is largely made up of Councillors but other officials, including the Borough Surveyor, are also present.

During the second half of the 20th century, television took over as the main leisure activity. Sadly, this, together with the internet and the advent of computer games, has resulted in many people staying within their home environment to pursue their leisure activities – something which would have been unthinkable to the Gateshead residents of time past to whom leisure was very much an 'outside the home' activity.

Chapter Nine
Nights Out

Nights out in Gateshead largely revolved around visiting pubs, cinemas and theatres. There were a variety of all three to choose from but for men in particular, a night out was about one thing only – a visit to the pub.

Public Houses

There were certainly lots of public houses available for the Gateshead drinker – he had no shortage of hostelries from which to choose! A stroll up the High Street in 1901 would have involved him passing 28 different drinking establishments – and that doesn't count those in the numerous small streets and alleys running off the High Street. Altogether, in central Gateshead alone at this time, there were 106 public houses. Few of these remain today but the names of those lost to us evoke an altogether different era – an era dominated by the industries men were employed in, with names like the Patent Hammer, the Steam Boat and the Glassmakers Arms, or famous people (real or imaginary) such as the Lord Nelson or the Robinson Crusoe. The Goat inn on Bottle Bank hid a surprise for the unwary drinker, as here it was said a man could be accused of being drunk, and tried for being drunk, without ever leaving the building – upstairs in the inn, Justices from the Court of Durham held meetings every Saturday while the Borough courts were held every Tuesday and Friday.

A sad looking Steamboat Inn photographed just before demolition in 1926.

The Goat Inn photographed just before demolition in 1926.

In the pubs, men could drink their beer (a much safer option than what passed for 'fresh' water in 19th century Gateshead!) to assuage their thirst after a hard day or night's work. Pubs were the preserve of the male and were often forbidden to women although ironically, women were allowed in to serve the men, and a number of women ran their own establishments. When women were bold enough to enter, they were often confined to the snug – usually a small corner separated from the main bar. Here they could sup their half of stout or ginger beer.

Many pubs were purpose built in all manner of styles, from the grand, such as the Queen's Head on Bottle Bank, to the

Male and female staff in The Magpie, Derwentwater Road in the 1920s.

purely functional often found on street corners such as the Globe on Pipewellgate. The Queen's Head was a substantial establishment with Hannah Murray one of its notable owners. Miss Murray reigned supreme during the 1860s and her 'dinners à la Russe' were widely praised. These became the style of 'meal out' we know today with various courses – unlike its predecessor, where a variety of food would be placed on the table with diners helping themselves liberally from communal plates. The Queen's Head was briefly used by the Town Council between 1867-70 when they had to decamp from their second town hall at Greenesfield (which was about to be flattened for the Team Valley Railway line). The Queen's Head however, grand though it was, was not the largest public house in Gateshead. That distinction belonged to the Grey Horse which often housed the Dispensary balls and early meetings of the Mechanics Institute. Thankfully, at the time of the Great Fire in 1854, it was too early in the morning for any drinkers, which was fortunate as a large stone was hurled 400 yards through the roof of this public house!

Over time, some pubs were rebuilt. Sometimes this was for the sake of modernisation as in the Dun Cow at the bottom of the High Street which was rebuilt twice. This photograph shows the interior of the first rebuild with its magnificent Tudor ceiling which had been rescued from the original building.

Sometimes a building had to be rebuilt because of accidental damage. The image below shows the Half Moon Inn which had to be rebuilt after a steam tram, rather too enthusiastically driven, took the corner at high speed and wrecked the previous building. The new building contained a restaurant and a hotel on the first and second floors.

The Half Moon (the Queen's Head is lower down Bottle Bank) in the 1930s.

The 19th century was seen as the period of expansion of hotels, inns, public houses and it saw the introduction of beer houses which could be opened by anyone for an annual licence of two guineas. They were an attempt by the government to increase competition between brewers and wean people away from other more injurious drinks such as gin (often called 'mothers ruin'). However, even in the 19th century some public houses were being demolished. Examples include the Black Bull on Bottle Bank which, at one time Gateshead's most noted coaching inn, disappeared when Snowball's shop was built while the Masons Arms (*right*) disappeared to make way for the Metropole Theatre on the High Street.

Unlike the 19th century, the 20th century was generally a period of decline as magistrates began to reduce the number of licensed establishments, particularly the beer houses. For example

The corner of High Street and Jackson Street in 1886. The Mason's Arms is shown at the very right of the photograph.

in 1906, nine out of 10 licences up for renewal were refused by the magistrates. These included the Burton House (Bottle Bank), the Blue Bell Inn (Bridge Street), the Bird Inn (Oakwellgate) and the Foresters Arms (East Street) which all closed. Because of these restrictions, when the Springfield Hotel opened in 1938, its licence had to be transferred from the Old Mill Inn which stood at the corner of West Street and Jackson Street. The building was later demolished and a new Co-op building was constructed on its site.

Others were demolished for different reasons. The Lord Nelson had to go when it was in the way of a traffic improvement scheme in the 1960s and both the Steamboat and the Goat Inn (*see page 88*) which had stood on Bottle Bank since the 17th century, had to be sacrificed for the construction of the Tyne Bridge.

Many of the pubs which have now disappeared from the Gateshead landscape were fairly poor specimens and often situated in the Gateshead slums. There was no need to appeal to the 'up market' clientele here! Good examples were the Barge Inn shown right or the Globe Inn (*below*) – where a pint of Alloa Ale could be bought for threepence. Pubs like these were strictly for the lower working classes.

One building, still very much with us today, was the unusually shaped Central Hotel (*right*) built in 1854 as business premises for Alderman John Potts, a spirit merchant. As the building plot was triangular, its shape resembles a coffin and this became its nickname.

There were some new pubs of course, many built to provide nights out for residents of the new housing estates which began to appear in Gateshead. For example the Gold Medal for the Chowdene estates, and the Jolly Miller (recently renamed the Stone Trough) for the Calderwood and Cromer Avenue areas of Low Fell.

Where you drank often depended on a variety of factors; location, clientele and 'class' were all important. The pubs which appealed to the working classes were not those the middle classes would frequent, and vice versa.

1938 saw the opening of the Springfield Hotel on Durham Road (*see photo on following page*). This was built as the first residential hotel in Gateshead at a cost of £30,000. At the opening ceremony, the Mayor, Ald Pickering, said, '*such a building as the Springfield Hotel tended to elevate a person's mind and led to sobriety.*'

The chairman of Gateshead Magistrates said, '*I think we can almost banish any thoughts of drunkenness. A man who will get drunk in such a place as this does not deserve to enter.*' Sadly this building went into receivership in 2009 and was later demolished.

With so many public houses to choose from, it is not surprising that drunkenness was a common offence in Gateshead. However, the Gateshead drunk was regarded with some tolerance – the Gateshead Observer reported in 1851 that they *'are not disorderly in their cups, but go pretty quietly along the street when drunk.'* 1924 proved to be a peak year for drunkenness when 766 charges were made. During the 19th century, in an effort to lead men away from the evils of drink, temperance bars were established. One such was the short lived British Workman, based in the former Institute building on Durham Road at Low Fell. Generally however, and for obvious reasons, these did not seem to appeal to many drinkers!

The Springfield Hotel on the right with the Shipcote Cinema on the left in 1950.

Theatres and Cinemas

Not everyone who fancied a night out wanted, or was able to go to, a public house. For these people, the attractions of the theatre were obvious. The Gateshead theatre goers of the early to mid 19th century didn't have any permanent venues to visit however. Troupes of players would come to Gateshead and hire any large space that was suitable, such as the long room at the New Cannon on Durham Road in Low Fell or Methuen's Long Room on the High Street. There were two early music halls in Gateshead but these were short lived. The People's Music Hall opened on Bottle Bank in 1874 but only lasted six years. Another – the Alexandra Music Hall in Oakwellgate – was closed on account of *'an unseemly performance'* after only a year! Oakwellgate also housed a temporary theatre which was sometimes used for pantomimes or by travelling players.

Equally short lived was Tudor's Empire Circus, held in a wooden building at the end of Sunderland Road which could house around 2,000 people. South Shields audiences had been the first to experience the delights of this circus but after running there for two seasons, the building was dismantled and brought to Gateshead where it opened in 1894. The owner was William Tudor, who performed juggling whilst riding a horse bare back. However, within two years, Tudor had sold the building which later seems to have become the Standard Theatre – a venue occasionally used for boxing matches (*see page 83*).

But this circus was a 'one off' and, pre-television, entertainment was found in the theatre and later the cinema. These opened up fantasy dreamworlds – worlds populated by heroes, beautiful heroines and, of course, villains. They provided somewhere where everyone could go – regardless of their income – and, for a few hours, enjoy pure escapism. Like the pubs, some cinemas and theatres catered for the working classes while others held more appeal to the better off. But most of them had a variety of prices to suit all pockets from the cheapest seats (often in the pits) to the expensive in the private boxes.

It was not until 1882 that Gateshead got its first permanent theatre when a former Methodist chapel on the High Street was converted to a Hall of Varieties. Six years later it was taken over by Frederick Stein and called the Theatre Royal. While it never rivalled its Newcastle namesake, it does seem to have been fairly successful, until a disaster at a pantomime performance on Boxing Day 1891 led to a temporary closure.

The Theatre Royal Disaster, 26th December 1891

This was a day that many of the poorer children looked forward to as they were given free tickets to see the annual pantomime. As the curtain rose, crowds of excited children were packed into the gallery seats at the top of the theatre. They were soon transfixed by the colourful costumes and the exotic stage sets, and to begin with all was well. Suddenly there was a cry of 'Fire, fire' which resulted in immediate panic. Children were quickly manhandled down to the ground floor where there was an immediate rush for the exit. Unfortunately, there was only one door, used as both entrance and exit, which opened inwards. In the rush, children were trampled underfoot with the result that nine children and the young doorkeeper were crushed to death. It was later discovered that a young boy, in an effort to search for a penny he had dropped, lit a match which set fire to a pile of rubbish.

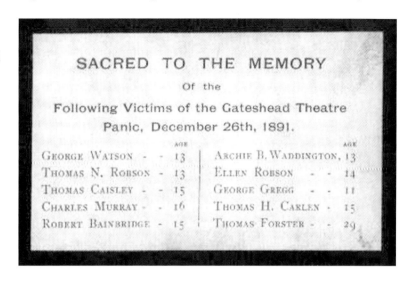

SACRED TO THE MEMORY

Of the

Following Victims of the Gateshead Theatre Panic, December 26th, 1891.

	AGE		AGE
GEORGE WATSON	13	ARCHIE B. WADDINGTON	13
THOMAS N. ROBSON	13	ELLEN ROBSON	14
THOMAS CAISLEY	15	GEORGE GREGG	11
CHARLES MURRAY	16	THOMAS H. CARLEN	15
ROBERT BAINBRIDGE	15	THOMAS FORSTER	29

Ironically, only two buckets of water were needed to extinguish the flames.

In 1894 (by which time it had been re-named the Queen's Theatre), the theatre was taken over by Weldon Watts, a theatre impresario, and managed to do well. However, it wasn't big enough for Watts' ambitions and he was soon planning a new, larger, theatre. This turned out to be the Metropole which was Gateshead's largest theatre and could hold 2,500 people. It was built on the site of the former Masons Arms at the junction of Jackson Street and the High Street (*see page 90*). To the Gateshead theatregoer, this building must have presented a sumptuous appearance with its marble staircase complete with brass hand rails and its ceiling, liberally festooned with cherubs among clouds.

There were separate lavatories for ladies and gentlemen (a sign of a 'classy' establishment!) and the building was heated by hot water pipes and lit by electricity. The theatre opened on 28th September 1896 with a performance of 'The Sign of the Cross' (a very successful and new play) by a touring company.

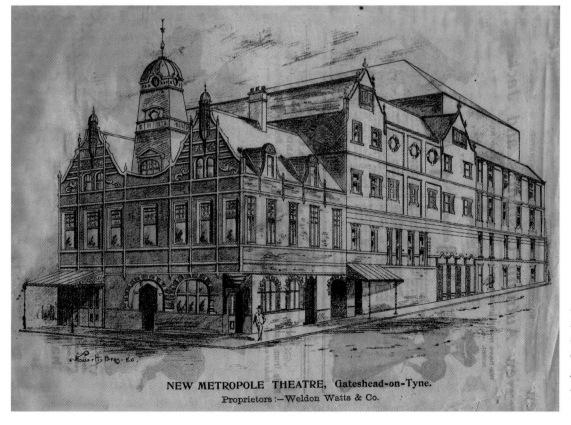

NEW METROPOLE THEATRE, Gateshead-on-Tyne.
Proprietors:—Weldon Watts & Co.

Left: Architect's drawing of the planned Metropole Theatre.

But within a few years, another theatre was to compete for audiences. This was the King's Theatre, an unusual fan shaped building due to its position at the High Street junction with Sunderland Road (this position ultimately meant it was in the way of the new A1 viaduct and it was demolished in 1968). Like the Metropole, this was also ornately decorated and could seat over 2,000 people. It opened in 1905 with a performance of 'Floradora' and its first pantomime was 'Aladdin and his magical lamp' (*below*) – the same pantomime which effectively saw the temporary demise of the Theatre Royal in 1891. It starred Miss Leonora Grieve (a popular actress in the 1900s) as Aladdin, and 'Little Britton' described as 'the smallest comedian in the world'. The King's was meant to run as a high class theatre by hiring the best London companies. However, this ambition remained unfulfilled as Gateshead was always outside the main theatre circuit. Instead, it became the home of visiting stock companies (10 are shown in this programme right).

In 1918, the theatre changed its name to the Empire and some big names did come here, albeit often before they had really made a name for themselves. These included Charlie Chaplin, who appeared as part of Fred Karno's 'Humming birds' troupe, and Harry Houdini, the escapologist. Marie Lloyd, who was a great music hall star, made her last appearance in a northern theatre at the Gateshead Empire in 1922.

The Queen's Theatre (which had became the Hippodrome in 1914) also attracted a variety of music hall stars such as Hetty King, the male impersonator, and G.H. Elliott – 'The Chocolate Coloured Coon'.

However, Gateshead's theatres were never really successful. They missed out on the big shows and many of the major stars.

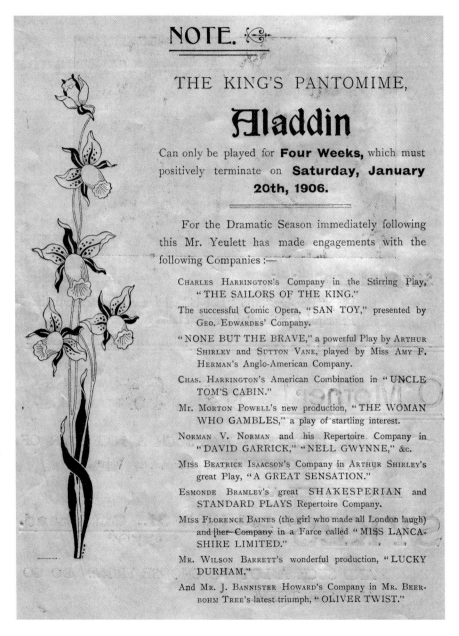

NOTE.

THE KING'S PANTOMIME,

Aladdin

Can only be played for **Four Weeks,** which must positively terminate on **Saturday, January 20th, 1906.**

For the Dramatic Season immediately following this Mr. Yeulett has made engagements with the following Companies :—

CHARLES HARRINGTON's Company in the Stirring Play, "THE SAILORS OF THE KING."

The successful Comic Opera, "SAN TOY," presented by GEO. EDWARDES' Company.

"NONE BUT THE BRAVE," a powerful Play by ARTHUR SHIRLEY and SUTTON VANE, played by Miss AMY F. HERMAN's Anglo-American Company.

CHAS. HARRINGTON's American Combination in "UNCLE TOM'S CABIN."

Mr. MORTON POWELL's new production, "THE WOMAN WHO GAMBLES," a play of startling interest.

NORMAN V. NORMAN and his Repertoire Company in "DAVID GARRICK," "NELL GWYNNE," &c.

MISS BEATRICE ISAACSON's Company in ARTHUR SHIRLEY's great Play, "A GREAT SENSATION."

ESMONDE BRAMLEY's great SHAKESPERIAN and STANDARD PLAYS Repertoire Company.

MISS FLORENCE BAINES (the girl who made all London laugh) and her Company in a Farce called "MISS LANCASHIRE LIMITED."

Mr. WILSON BARRETT's wonderful production, "LUCKY DURHAM."

And Mr. J. BANNISTER HOWARD's Company in Mr. BEERBOHM TREE's latest triumph, "OLIVER TWIST."

So, how could the theatre managers achieve good audiences and success at the box office? The answer lay in the moving picture show.

By 1899, audiences at both the Queen's and the Metropole had seen early moving pictures. 'Downey's living pictures of the South African war' was shown at the Metropole and audiences at the Town Hall (a venue often used for entertainment) had seen a similar film about the same war. These were primitive films but cinema technology improved and by 1907, a night out at the King's Theatre might have included viewing the heavyweight championship boxing match of the same year, when Tommy Burns knocked out 'Gunner' Moir.

These early films were shown using a bioscope – a type of early film projector – which could be taken around from venue to venue. One of these was taken to St Paul's Church on Askew Road to show a film called 'Courtship'. Unfortunately, the film was stopped halfway through by the vicar who objected to a kissing scene in it as *'unfit to be shown'*!

In 1909 Gateshead people were probably the first on Tyneside to view films in a purpose built cinema when the Ravensworth (nicknamed the 'Rats') opened in Bank Street. The cinema was well placed to achieve high audience figures as it was situated right in the middle of tightly packed terraced houses. However it was a fairly basic building with wooden forms in the pit and green corduroy tip-up seats in the stalls. It did however, have its own orchestra and on Sunday evenings was scheduled to have concerts of sacred music. This was a ploy often used to persuade magistrates that picture halls were 'a good thing'.

But Gateshead film fans were soon to have a much grander building. This was the Palace on Sunderland Road, often referred to as Black's Palace after the owner, George Black. It was designed both as a picture and variety theatre and when it opened in 1909 was described as '*this up to date Electrical Theatre*'.

In contrast, the next cinema to open was 'Lloyd's Living Pictures' on the High Street, built originally with at least a degree of comfort in mind, although it wasn't long before it had acquired (for obvious reasons) the unfortunate nickname of Loppy Lloyds! Within a year it was re-named the Empress but the nickname stuck (as did the fleas who seem to have been permanent residents!).

Low Fell residents got their first (and very poor) cinema in 1911 when the Coronation opened above four shops

Interior of the Empress in 1956.

on Durham Road. This was never a success and within four years had closed, becoming Gateshead's shortest lived cinema. Apart from its size (small) and comfort (poor), the main reason for its closure was the fact that a much better picture house opened on Durham Road in 1911. This was the Shipcote designed to provide '*high class family entertainment*'. The manager, Johnny Snell, invariably wore full evening dress with a silk top hat.

Left: Shipcote staff pictured about 1914.

By the time the First World War began, Gateshead had seven cinemas together with the Town Hall, the Metropole and the King's Theatre, all of which featured occasional film

shows. By the time the Second World War began, it had 16 cinemas of which four, the Rex, the Ritz, Black's Regal and the Capitol, were opened during the boom time for cinema viewing in the 1930s. The day that Black's Regal opened in 1937 saw a crowd of almost 2,000 gathered on the High Street to see the opening performed by Britain's then highest paid cinema star, Gracie Fields, who cut short a holiday in Biarritz to do so (*right*). In a later letter, Gracie remembered feeling guilty that she was '*swanning around in a swanky limousine*' while the crowds were standing in the pouring rain.

Falling audiences at the Metropole Theatre had prompted its alteration to a cinema (it was renamed the Scala cinema in 1919), and the Hippodrome was burnt out in a fire in 1922 so, by 1930, only the King's Theatre, which had been renamed the Empire in 1918, was still concentrating on live shows. In 1938, Hughie Green (who went on to become a famous, and later infamous, television star) brought his own all-children cast concert party called 'Hughie Green and his Gang' to the Empire. Other stars who appeared at the Empire at various times included Stanley Holloway, Tommy Trinder and Gracie Fields. In a letter written some years later, Gracie Fields wrote '*I look back on the Gateshead Empire Theatre with grateful thanks as being one of the big stepping stones on my way to stardom.*' The Empire held annual benefit concerts to finance the holiday camps held at Blackhall Rocks for the poor children of Gateshead (*see also page 29*).

Hughie Green's Band at the Empire with the Mayor of Gateshead W.J. Pickering.

Members of Gateshead Operatic and Dramatic Society in their production of 'The Pirates of Penzance' in 1936.

Another venue, Gateshead Town Hall (from the very beginning, its facilities included a hall with a stage) also hosted live performances – sometimes these were amateur productions (*as in the photo above*) and many school productions (and speech nights) were held here. The photograph below shows a scene from 'Time Gentlemen Please' performed here for an audience of unemployed people by the Northern Vaudeville Company.

But it was the cinemas which were now really attracting the crowds and 'going to the pictures' became, for many people at least, a regular activity. In 1920, the Coatsworth was extended to incorporate waiting rooms and lounges, which meant customers no longer had to stand in a queue outside waiting to buy a ticket. Many cinemas, including the Coatsworth, also operated an 'early doors' policy. This meant that if you were willing to pay a little extra, you could have a choice of unreserved seats.

'Time Gentlemen Please', 28th March 1931.

All cinemas had children's matinees – and for some you could get in if you brought jam jars. One of these was the Empress and another was the Askew. The Askew (which was run by a grocer, Cecil Horn) allowed children in for nothing – provided their mother had spent 2/6 at his shop. Most cinemas shared reels with others to cut down on cost so, if you missed a film at your favourite cinema, you could often catch it at another. The Shipcote, for example, was twinned with the Askew which meant reels of films were carried between the two halls by runners whose wages were 8d a night plus 4d tram fare while the Palace on

Sunderland Road was twinned with the Scala and both often showed the same pictures as the Shipcote.

Until the arrival of the 'talkies' in the late 1920s, some cinemas had their own orchestras who would play music throughout the film and also at intervals when the reels were being changed. One of the best orchestras was at the Shipcote – which advertised their orchestra as '*If you desire the best, it's here; if it's here, it is the best.*' The tiny Askew cinema didn't have room for an orchestra but they had an alternative in Redvers Taylor, described as the 'wonder boy pianist'. In contrast, one of the largest orchestras was at the Coatsworth where their 'Coatsworth Grand Orchestra' had 15 players – generally speaking, the larger the orchestra, the better the status of the cinema.

The Bensham was the first cinema in Gateshead to show a talking picture. This was 'In Old Arizona' which audiences saw in 1929. The talkies effectively saw off the need for an orchestra – Joseph Chapman, the leader of the orchestra at the Classic on Kells Lane, was so upset when given two weeks notice in 1930 that he vowed never to watch a talking picture. However, for many years, music did remain a feature of many cinemas and was usually played between the films. Electric organs were often installed as the photograph right of the organ at Black's Regal (later the Odeon) shows.

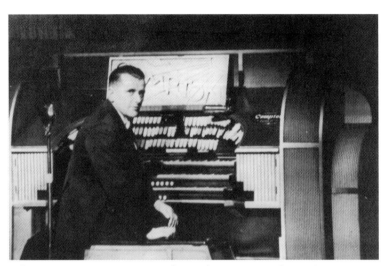

The Compton organ with Arthur Largerburg in 1937.

In 1946, the Empire Theatre became part of the Essoldo cinema chain. This was the first cinema in Gateshead to screen 3D and CinemaScope films (widescreen films) as the advert right for April 1956 shows. Incidentally, the Scala may have been the only cinema in the country to show CinemaScope films by rear projection.

'The Man Who Never Was' starring Clifton Webb and Gloria Grahame.

In the 1950s, cinema audience figures began to drop as television became more affordable and obtainable. In an effort to attract new audiences, The Odeon's café was transferred into a Victor Sylvester dance studio but gradually, cinema managers discovered that 'nights out' were becoming 'nights in'. Between 1956-60, seven cinemas closed. This included The Scala which, as the newspaper cutting left from the Gateshead Post for 15th October 1956 shows, was described as '*The Ghost Theatre is vanishing*' – a sad end to a once grand building. By 1967, only the Odeon and the Classic (formerly the Capitol in Low Fell) were still operating. In 1975, the once stylish Art Deco Odeon was converted to a bingo hall and in 1987, Gateshead's last survivor, the Classic, finally closed its doors.

A LAST LOOK AT THE SCALA

ONCE THE METROPOLE THEATRE, then the Scala Cinema —but now workmen are stripping it down. Soon it will be used as a warehouse.

THE GHOST THEATRE IS VANISHING . . .

Stripped to make room for stores

However, one building has consistently continued to provide audiences with a night out in Gateshead – The Little Theatre on Saltwell View. The theatre opened on 10th October 1943 with a performance of Shakespeare's 'A Midsummer Night's Dream' by the resident company, the Progressive Players, and with music performed by the Bensham Settlement Orchestra. The opening ceremony was performed by Mary Gunn, Gateshead's first lady Mayor and over 70 years later, the theatre continues to attract full houses. Initially, six plays were performed each year but since 1967, 10 plays have been produced annually. The theatre was a huge step forward for the Progressive Players who until then had to perform their plays in the Westfield Hall – on a moveable stage which had to be frequently dismantled when the hall was used for other purposes.

It has to be said however, that audiences on their 'nights out' have not always behaved well. Apparently, at the Ravensworth cinema, children would use the tip up seats to crack the shells of nuts, while at the Palladium, the pianist was frequently pelted with apple cores if the audience didn't like the film. Sadly, the main reason for the closure of one Gateshead cinema – the Bensham – was that vandalism increased during the 1950s, and rowdy behaviour and regular seat slashing became an unfortunate feature.

Fortunately, rowdy behaviour does not seem to have troubled the Progressive Players overmuch. Their programmes of the 1930s for the Westfield Hall merely carried a polite request *'In the interests of the people behind you please remove your hat.'*

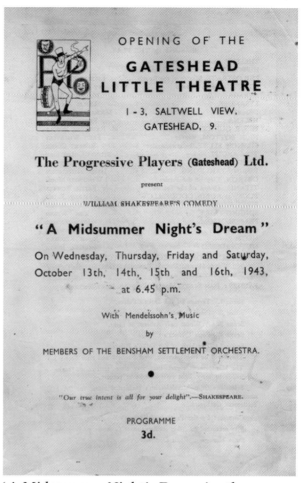

'A Midsummer Night's Dream' – the Progressive Players' first production at the Little Theatre.

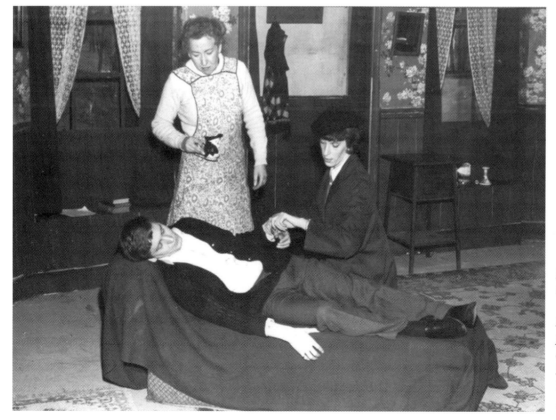

Left: A scene from 'Night Must Fall' performed at the Little Theatre in 1965.

Chapter Ten
Under Threat – Gateshead at War

Until the 20th century, wars seem to have had little impact on Gateshead. We know very little about the effect of the Boer war here although there are two Boer War memorials – one in Saltwell Park and another on Durham Road, Low Fell. Of the 900 men who enlisted, 77 never returned. The South African War memorial in Saltwell Park is a tall obelisk surmounted by the Angel of Peace with the names of the fallen listed under the various regiments in which they served, whilst on Durham Road is a statue of a Boer War soldier erected to the memory of Sergeant Crone (a Low Fell man) and his four colleagues in 1903.

Saltwell Park Boer War memorial unveiled on 11th November 1905.

Durham Road memorial.

The First World War

The First World War however, did have a major effect on Gateshead life from recruitment to the return of the many men who served. Before the war had even begun, the colours of the 9th Battalion of the Durham Light Infantry (often referred to as the Gateshead Battalion) were laid up in St Mary's church.

The DLI's main recruitment centre was the drill hall in Burt Terrace but this became just one of many. A recruiting office was opened on the High Street but once the Derby scheme, introduced in 1915, came into force, these premises weren't big enough and recruitment moved to the Town Hall. The Derby scheme meant that men who voluntarily registered ('attested') would be called up only when necessary, with married men informed they would be called up only when the supply of single men was exhausted.

Gun carriage outside Kells Lane school, 1917.

Men were classified in groups according to their year of birth and called up when that group was required. There was praise for the Mayor, Alderman Wardill for his efforts in recruitment.

However, the increase in the number of recruits meant a problem with their accommodation. They had to be housed somewhere whilst undergoing instruction in the use of guns and drill and public buildings such as Kells Lane Board School were often used.

THE FAITHFUL DURHAMS

ON **M**ONDAY **N**IGHT

OCTOBER 19th, the performance of

THE

COUNT OF LUXEMBOURG

Will be under the Distinguished Patronage
of Colonel Kenyon-Slaney, D.L.I.; Colonel the
Hon. W, L. Vane, D.L.I.; Officers and N.C.O.'s of
the "Faithful Durhams," stationed at Newcastle.

For this occasion a Patriotic Scena will be added,
including the well-known Song:

"SONS OF THE MOTHERLAND"

AND

COLONEL VANE WILL ADDRESS THE AUDIENCE
ON RECRUITING.

MONDAY NIGHT

AT THE

KING'S, GATESHEAD

R. KELLY, Printer, West Street, Gateshead.

9th Bn. Durham Light Infantry Regiment

(FAITHFUL DURHAMS).

Headquarters:
DRILL HALL, BURT TERRACE, ALEXANDRA ROAD,
GATESHEAD-UPON-TYNE.

AND AT

FELLING. :: BLAYDON. :: CHOPWELL.

Your King and Country Need You.
—400—
SMART MEN,
AGE 19 TO 38,

Are wanted to join this Battalion **AT ONCE** for Foreign
Service for the duration of the War.

MEN, COME AND JOIN!

Apply to the following Drill Halls where all particulars will
be given by the Officer in charge—

GATESHEAD—Drill Hall, Burt Terrace.
BLAYDON—Drill Hall.
CHOPWELL—Drill Hall.
FELLING—Drill Hall.

"GOD SAVE THE KING."

R. KELLY, PRINTER, GATESHEAD.

Audiences may have been surprised to see that the performance of the Count of Luxembourg on 19th October 1914 at the King's Theatre would include both a new song and a recruitment lecture!

Posters liked this resulted in a flood of enlistments.

In 1915, a Volunteer Training Corps was established at Gateshead. Similar to the Home Guard of the Second World War, men who had attested under the Derby Scheme, were encouraged to join for drill practice. Their headquarters were at Elmgrove Terrace and the men soon became a common site in Saltwell Park where they practised weekly drills. Blockading of British ports by German vessels began in 1915 and this eventually led to severe food shortages and ultimately to rationing (though this was not imposed until 1918).

The same year saw the first Zeppelin raids over Britain. Fortunately, Gateshead was unaffected by these but, in common with other towns, had to impose a form of blackout. Lights had to be dimmed or dowsed (complete blackout was only necessary when Zeppelins were sighted in the area) and failure to comply resulted in prosecutions. Only half of each street in Gateshead was lighted. Not everyone was happy with this however and one very indignant letter written to the local newspaper in October 1915 by a munitions worker who had injured himself by slipping on a banana skin in an unlit street stated '*I trust for the public safety, banana eaters will dispose of the waste on the roadway.*'

As recruitment continued, women gradually took over many of the jobs done by men and tram conductresses became a familiar sight on the streets of Gateshead (*right*). From 1915, it was also possible to find female street sweepers – described in the press as '*sturdy specimens of womanhood. They are quite capable … of wielding the broom with vigour.*' Saltwell Park also saw women employed as gardeners for the first time.

On 7th May 1915, an international tragedy occurred which resulted in a night-time of mob activity in Gateshead's shopping streets. The Lusitania, a large passenger liner carrying civilians, was sunk by German U-boats. This caused an outcry and resulted in extreme anti-Germanic feeling in towns throughout the North East. German pork

butchers, even those who had already anglicised their names were a particular target. In Gateshead, these included shops owned by J. George Cook, Dietz and Egner on the High Street and Charles Seitz on Askew Road West. The attack on Cook's was described vividly in the press. Between 9-10 pm the shop was completely emptied of its contents, a piano was thrown from an upstairs window and, due to the size of the crowds,

Above: A policeman guards J. George Cook.

Left: Crowds gather outside Egner's butchers.

the police were powerless to stop activities. Only stopping trams caused a pause in proceedings but once they went on their way, mob activity began again. The 37 claims resulting from these riots meant that the Council had to pay £1,030 to cover them although payment wasn't made until January 1916.

The Armenian flag day was held in response to news of the Ottoman government's systematic extermination of its minority Armenian residents.

From 1915, flag days became a regular feature of street life in Gateshead. There were flag days for Armenians, Russian and Polish Jews, and the French, but also more local ones such as those for the Tyneside Scottish regiment and a pansy day which was held for the Missions to Seamen. More poignantly, in 1917 a flag day was held for the blinded soldiers and sailors at St Dunstan's established in 1915.

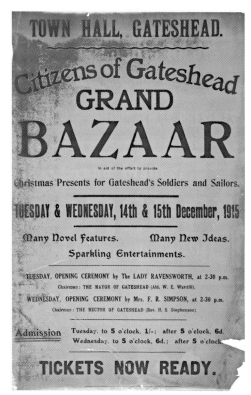

There was no shortage of gifts for servicemen. Within a month of its formation in November 1915, the Gateshead Association of Voluntary Workers for Soldiers and Sailors had sent 800 mufflers and 1,250 pairs of mittens to the War Office. Frequent initiatives took place which resulted in a constant stream of activities for the war effort. One of the major events was the Grand Bazaar (*right*). This was held at the Town Hall in December 1915. Described as '*a golden opportunity for all who delight in honouring the brave*', the idea behind it was to send a Christmas parcel to every Gateshead man serving in the army or navy. The bazaar was opened by Lady Ravensworth, whose husband was the president of the committee.

Each man received a Christmas card (provided free by Henderson & Birkett of Hill Street) together with gifts of chocolates and cigarettes. To ensure no man was missed out, every house in Gateshead was visited to find out who was away serving. Everyone was asked for money 'A copper or two from each house ... would ensure an acceptable gift for the men.'

Inmates of the workhouse were not forgotten as they had their own Christmas celebrations and tucked into roast beef, followed by plum pudding and mineral waters. Pipes were provided for the men by Mr Smith of Pipewellgate whilst women got tea and sugar. Those in the hospital were given a lighter diet of rabbit, chicken and plum pudding and everyone had spiced tea cakes for tea.

It wasn't long before Gateshead experienced the sight of wounded soldiers, many of whom were housed in the local wartime VAD hospitals established, firstly at Whinney House and then in 1916, an offshoot at Saltwell Towers. Both were run jointly by the Red Cross and St John Ambulance Brigade. Nine wards were created at Saltwell Towers which could hold 50 beds. The men weren't allowed to stay idle and were encouraged to take up crafts such as woodwork or embroidery. Enough were occupied doing needlework for Whinney House to hold an exhibition of the men's work with prizes in December 1917.

Soldiers and nurses outside Whinney House VAD hospital.

Seats marked '*for the use of wounded soldiers only*' began to appear in Saltwell Park and two ambulances were presented by Sir James Knott, the shipping magnate, to the park to transport wounded soldiers to the hospital.

As the war progressed it became apparent that Britain was in for the long haul and might need to defend itself at home. This resulted in the establishment of new rifle clubs in Gateshead. Although the idea was nothing new (a number of clubs already existed including one just for ladies), a schoolboys' miniature rifle club was set up for boys under 11 by Inspector Elliott of Gateshead police.

In 1916, Britain faced a severe food crisis. Merchant ships were being blockaded by German U-boats and imports of grain dried up. This meant a new act 'The Cultivation of Lands order' which led to a search for suitable sites in Gateshead for use as allotments. Potatoes were planted around the South African War memorial in Saltwell Park and tenants of Saltwell cemetery gardens were allowed to keep pigs and poultry for the duration of the war. The people of Gateshead however, don't seem to have been particularly enthusiastic gardeners and in January 1917, this lack of enthusiasm was being remarked upon. Building sites at Joicey Road, Albert Drive, Brighton Road and Field House Road were all earmarked for allotments with the hope that the spring weather would bring out these reluctant gardeners. Supplies of raw sugar were also in short supply due to the U-boat blockade and in Gateshead, many of the local shopkeepers voluntarily imposed sugar rationing and allotted sugar in direct relation to the size of each family.

The 25th May 1916, saw the introduction of the Military Service Act which meant voluntary registration (under the Derby scheme) was stopped and conscription began. Within a month, a large number of cases were coming before the Gateshead War tribunal. Gateshead's tribunal was regarded as very effective – they ruled on a surprisingly high number of cases with most men being ordered to undertake non-combative service. The same month also saw the formation of the War Savings Association which organised an open air campaign to kick off proceedings. By April 1917, £114,591 19s had been invested. Lord Kitchener had described these war certificates as 'the bullets of silver and bronze.' (right)

In contrast to that of 1915, Christmas 1916 was a bleak affair with the Mayor of Gateshead, Councillor John Maccoy (the chair of Gateshead War Association), appealing to everyone to refrain from Christmas and New Year festivities and suggesting that they buy 15/6 war savings certificates as presents.

Gateshead's fire station in Swinburne Street got a new motor fire engine in 1917 (below). The impetus for this, however, was not necessarily improved speed and efficiency, but a result of the difficulties in obtaining suitable horses (most were requisitioned for the war effort) and also finding

the amount of hay necessary to feed the Council's 450 horses.

Food shortages had reached such a peak by 1917 that the question of communal feeding stations arose. The Salvation Army opened the first public food kitchen in Gateshead at 316 Askew Road although there was no opportunity to sit down and eat a meal and people were asked to bring their own dishes and plates to take their food away. Opened daily between 12 noon and 2 pm, 200 dinners were prepared each day. On the first day, all had gone in the first 45 minutes! In May 1917, a Local Food Control Committee was formed (not disbanded until September 1920) with Gateshead being given an allowance from the Food Ministry of £457 10s based on a population of 130,000. At the first meeting of 1918, the press reported that the Mayor had said 'Food was a serious problem. Not many of the Council looked as if they were rationed ... but he advised them to ration themselves severely.' On 7th February 1918 it was decided to establish a communal kitchen at Gateshead.

Towards the end of the war, anti-German feeling was so strong it led to the renaming of two Gateshead streets. Berlin Street and Frankfurt Street in the Redheugh area of town, now became Clasper and Chambers Streets although neighbouring 'allied' streets such as Brussels, remained unaltered.

Finally, on 19th July 1919, a national Peace Day was declared and the war was officially at an end. The Windmill Hills saw a service of thanksgiving after which the Mayor of Gateshead held a special luncheon at the Town Hall with salmon, chicken and ham on the menu as well as trifle and jellies. This was then followed by a fete in Saltwell Park where the Mayoress, Miss Daisy Maccoy, planted an oak tree in commemorate victory and peace. Celebrations in the park continued until late in the evening then, at 11 pm, flares were lit at Sheriff Hill which burned until midnight.

Victory celebrations were often epitomised by burning an effigy of the Kaiser, which was usually stuck on the top of a bonfire for the purpose. This happened at the Bensham workhouse on 24th July 1919 after the inmates had partaken of a roast beef dinner followed by games, dancing and a concert. It was also a feature at the Victory tea held in King Edward Street the previous day.

Victory teas were many and varied but the Chief Constable proved an unpopular figure in Gateshead when he ordered that from August 1919, no more were to be held. In a press notice he explained that one woman had been found drunk and incapable in Lambton Street after returning from a victory tea, whilst trees and bushes on Windmill Hills had been desecrated to provide decoration for street parties. He ended by saying that he had cautioned a number of children about begging in the streets for the teas. The ban resulted in a storm of protest but to no avail – victory teas were no more.

A 1919 victory tea in Riddle Street, Bensham.

Dellow's coffin is taken from his parent's house in High Street West.

Burials of men who had died as a result of injuries at home were a continuing feature throughout the war as the number of war graves can testify in Saltwell and Gateshead East cemeteries. However, one particular funeral touched the hearts of the local populace.

Richard Dellow was the son of a Gateshead dentist. He enlisted in the 18th Northumberland Fusiliers during October 1914, was soon promoted to sergeant and went overseas with the regiment in January 1916. He took part in the battle of the Somme as a result of which he was awarded a commission for gallantry in February 1917 and later transferred to the 19th Fusiliers. He was invalided home with trench fever which ultimately led to heart problems and he died in a private nursing home in August 1919. The service was held at Holy Trinity Church which was followed by an interment at Gateshead East cemetery. Hundreds stood in silent tribute as the cortege with the coffin draped in the Union flag and surmounted by Dellow's regimental cap, wended its way along the High Street (*see left*).

After Gateshead had settled back to peace conditions, plans were soon made for a war memorial to commemorate the fallen. 1,700 Gateshead men had been killed of which 986 had served in the 9th Battalion of the DLI – a battalion which gained more individual honours than any other unit in the British army. It was decided to erect this at Shipcote. The designer was John W. Spink of Kingston-on-Thames and it was built using Heworth Blue stone from the Tate Brown quarries by Alexander Pringle of Gateshead (who later built the Central Library) at a cost of £5,500. All the money was raised through public subscription – 9,232 people subscribed together with nearly 20,000 schoolchildren. The cenotaph was formally unveiled on 14th May 1922. Built in a classic cenotaph design a bronze panel depicts a warrior nine feet high depicting 'Manhood' in front of a cross. He is depicted in an attitude of defence, his hands lightly resting upon an unsheathed sword. The inscription '*Mors Janua Vitae*' means '*Death is the Gate of Life*'.

The unveiling of the war memorial, 14th May 1922 by General Sir Percy S. Wilkinson. Four of the men of 'The Durhams' wearing steel helmets stand at each corner.

The Second World War

Unlike the First World War, preparations for the Second World War were being made well ahead of the actual event with one councillor calling for action as early as 1936.

On 8th July 1938, South Dene Towers was formally opened as Gateshead's ARP headquarters. Six months later, a bomb proof ARP centre was constructed in the basement of the Borough Treasurer's Department. The control room was given two extra ceilings of reinforced concrete burster slabs which rested on 35 steel girders with their bases embedded in concrete. There was emergency lighting and the room was regarded as gas proof as far as possible. It was linked to the executive control room at South Dene Towers by a direct line. Gateshead's 70hp fire engine was regarded as the most powerful of its kind in the North of England.

September 1938 saw shelters being built to house 80,000 of Gateshead's population – this included one situated under the Town Hall. Gateshead estimated that to provide all the ARP shelters needed would cost £32,400 and they appealed against the government grant of 75%. Shelters were built in places where houses had no gardens – these included slum cleared areas, fields and other open spaces. Deep shelters were constructed in Saltwell Park, South Dene Towers and Bensham Terrace. In total, these were designed to accommodate between 3,000 – 4,000 people. One of the best air raid shelters in the north was the Shipley Gallery. The basement and storage room were reinforced with concrete and supported by strong wooden props and the whole building was barricaded by hundreds of sandbags.

Digging the air raid shelter in Saltwell Park.

The Team Valley Trading Estate became the site for the Home Office Regional Store. In a secret location on the

Valley, three million gas masks were stored for emergency distribution to the population of Northumberland and Durham. During July, a gas mask fitting census involving 1,400 gas masks was carried out by ARP wardens who visited every house taking a note of the number of inhabitants and the sizes of gas masks needed. By the end of the month, every inhabitant had been fitted for a gas mask. Little baby Lasky born at 13 Thomas Street in May 1940, made temporary history at least, by becoming the youngest person in the country (45 seconds old) to wear a gas respirator when she was popped in to one as a 'trial' by an enthusiastic ARP warden who lived two doors away.

A major recruiting drive was held on 9th May 1939 which was described as the biggest military parade for many years. Headed by a full military band, 700 members of the 9th DLI marched along Prince Consort Road. Addresses were given at Windmill Hills and also at the War Memorial at Shipcote.

Buildings soon began to be used for new purposes. The Presbyterian Church Hall in Durham Road became the temporary headquarters of the newly formed 3rd Anti-Aircraft Royal Army Service Corps

Wing Commander E.G. Hodsall, Inspector General of Air Raid Precautions, is shown the gas masks at the Team Valley store.

with a subsequent appeal going out in April 1939 for qualified motor drivers from artisans and clerks aged 25-50.

Some of Gateshead's large houses also became scenes of war time activity. As well as South Dene Towers described earlier, Briermede, a substantial house in Earl's Drive, was used as a temporary drill hall by the 234th Field Company of the Royal Engineers until their new drill hall was completed. Four hundred territorials met in this house so conditions would have been rather cramped to say the least! It was described in the press as *'anything but ideal'*.

Mayfield, another substantial house, became Gateshead's first refugee hostel for 12-15 students from Czechoslovakia and Germany who were studying at King's College Newcastle. Secretary of the committee to run the hostel was Ruth Dodds who, with two of her sisters would go on to found Gateshead's Little Theatre (*see page 99*) in 1943.

Churches and their associated buildings also had new uses. Holy Trinity vicarage was adapted at a cost of £600 for a war time nursery while pews were removed from Durham Road Presbyterian Church in order to make space for the storage of furniture from bomb damaged premises.

Six hundred steel 'Anderson' air raid shelters arrived on Tyneside in February 1939, of which 450 were designated for Gateshead. Unemployed labourers were employed to erect them but many householders refused to allow this preferring nice looking gardens over safety.

On 7th May 1939 the whole of Tyneside was involved in a black-out operation with various exercises carried out throughout the region. Between 1 am and 3 am it was planned that RAF planes would fly over Tyneside to attempt to distinguish landmarks in the area. However, fog settled in and the exercise had to be abandoned. The Mayor of Gateshead, who was meant to start a fire without being detected by official patrols, arrived at his destination – derelict chemical works in Park Road – only to discover spectators were already there! As the fire took hold, the engine belonging to the Auxiliary Fire Service was summoned. Unfortunately, the hose was too short and by the time a longer hose had been procured, the blaze was well away and eventually only extinguished with some difficulty.

Evacuation

Evacuation of school children was being planned long before war was declared. A full scale rehearsal was held on Monday 28th August 1939 with the 'real thing' happening on 2nd September. This was a major logistical exercise on a scale never before carried out and yet it was a success, albeit that, due to the 'phoney war', within six weeks over 25% of the evacuees had returned. Evacuation parties from schools proceeded in columns headed by a banner bearing the school name to either Gateshead West or Bensham train stations.

Smartly dressed Gateshead Secondary Schoolboys on their way to the station.

Most Gateshead children were evacuated to areas of North Yorkshire such as Richmond, Leyburn and Thirsk although some had rather shorter journeys to Darlington and Crook. Each child had one piece of hand luggage and wore a label with their name and that of their school. School equipment and heavy luggage was sent on later by freight train later. The first train left Gateshead West at 8.15 am bound for Richmond with 650 evacuees from Wrekenton Junior & Infants, St Oswald's and Shipcote boys. The last train left at 3.45 pm with children from Carr Hill Seniors, Juniors and Infants headed for Bishop Auckland. Altogether, 18,305 evacuees left Gateshead on this one day.

Day two of evacuation was reserved for mothers and babies, expectant mothers and sick and blind people. This was overseen by the recently formed Gateshead branch of the Women's Royal Voluntary Service (WRVS). Within the first year of their existence, they had filled in over 100,000 ration cards and raised £3,500 for the Red Cross – a record for the whole country. They went on to run the Citizen's Advice Bureau and a panel of

Young children with their gas masks and identity labels.

their members undertook to wash and darn half a dozen pairs of socks for soldiers and airmen each week.

Schools were closed at the start of the war and so most children were educated in home classes although some schools were opened in order for senior pupils to attend to collect homework. This caused major problems as the quickly returning evacuees had nowhere to go. In October 1939, Gateshead began a countrywide campaign to start re-opening schools in evacuation areas to take children off the streets. By January 1940, there were about 100 'parlour' schools operating

The Mayor Councillor William Pickering, with mothers and children prior to evacuation.

in the town and by April half time education was in operation.

Prior Street Infants School did their bit for the war effort by running their own Post Office and selling war savings stamps and were even filmed for Pathé News in the process.

Right: Evacuation from Gateshead West station, 2nd September 1939.

Helping with the War Effort

In May 1940, Anthony Eden, Secretary of State for War, announced the formation of the Local Defence Volunteers (subsequently called 'The Home Guard') and appealed for men aged between 17 and 65 to enrol in the force at their local police station. The original function was to watch for German parachutists and in Gateshead the force was nicknamed 'the parashooters'. Saltwell Park was frequently used for their drills, manoeuvres and training exercises. One hundred and twenty men enrolled within the first three hours – some of whom were First World War and even Boer War veterans.

During the first year of the war, Gateshead's streetscape took on a different look as railings were removed from outside properties – ostensibly for the war effort. Churches and even Saltwell Park also gave up supplies of metalwork. Opinion is divided as to whether this was ever actually used but what is certain is that far more iron was collected than was ever needed.

As rationing hit, people were encouraged to 'grow their own' using allotments – as with the First World War, extra sites were provided at various locations throughout Gateshead. Among these were 21 allotments at Rawling Road, 16 at South Dene Towers and 19 on Victoria Road. Saltwell Park also featured, with allotment holders here being provided with plants from the Parks Superintendent.

The 'British restaurant' movement also came to Gateshead and the Indo-Chinese Pavilion in Saltwell Park was transformed into one in 1943. These restaurants provided food for people who had run out of food rationing coupons.

In 1941 Gateshead 'adopted' a Spitfire. The Gateshead Spitfire began operational service in June 1941 and was sent to fighter squadron engaged in coastal defences and convoy escort duty. However, the following month, the Spitfire crashed and was so badly damaged it had to be withdrawn from operational service. Once repaired, it was posted to special flying duties with the RAF. In March 1943, it was withdrawn for an overhaul and was then involved in air sea rescue duties.

The Gateshead Spitfire.

Every year seemed to involve the people of Gateshead saving for something. War Weapons Week was the first major, national initiative in 1940 and certificates were sold from various Council owned buildings in Gateshead.

Gateshead 'adopted' its own destroyer – HMS Eskimo (built in 1936 at Vickers Armstrong, Elswick) during Warship Week held in February 1942. Gateshead raised £183,000 above the target figure of £500,000. (*Right: HMS Eskimo.*)

June 1943 saw Wings for Victory Week which had as a highlight, an RAF exhibition at the Shipley

Gallery. The week raised a staggering £818,563 – again, well above the target figure of £750,000 and began with a parade of representatives of HM Forces and Civil Defence Volunteers assembled near the Tyne Bridge. The programme for the week contained three dances, physical training displays by the Air Training Corps and bands in Saltwell Park plus a swimming gala at the Shipcote baths. The purpose of the week was to provide funds to purchase 12 Stirling four engined bombers.

The focus of Salute the Soldier Week in June 1944 was to clothe and equip three DLI battalions. The aim was to raise over £500,000 but once again, Gateshead raised well over this target figure (£650,000).

Not all news stories could be reported at the time but one which did make the local papers was the account of an auction in June 1943 when Lance Bombardier Smith brought home from Gibraltar a banana and a lemon and auctioned both in Saltwell Park, with the proceeds going to the RAF Benevolent Fund. The banana raised £5 1s and the lemon was purchased for a staggering £8!

There were some perks for servicemen on leave during the war. They were given free use of a bowling green in Saltwell Park so long as they were in uniform and wore suitable sandshoes or overshoes and in December 1939, a recreation room for forces was established at the former Old Mill Inn on West Street providing a variety of games whilst a canteen committee of 50 ladies worked in relays of six per day to produce cheap meals for the men.

As in the First World War, Flag Days became a feature of life in Gateshead although this time they seem to have been more focussed on home, rather than foreign, fund raising. The Red Cross and St John Ambulance held a flag day in June 1940, followed a few weeks later by the Newcastle Lord Mayor's and Evening Chronicle joint War Comforts Flag Day.

Victory In Europe Day was declared on 8th May 1945. Behind the scenes, Gateshead's Town Clerk, John Porter, had been quietly planning the celebrations. Special church services were held throughout Gateshead, the King's speech was broadcast from Saltwell Park and at 10 pm, a bonfire was lit at Moss Heap Quarry near Wrekenton.

And of course, from VE day onwards, the ubiquitous Victory Teas resurrected themselves with the Council allocating £625 for children's refreshments.

VE celebrations in Exeter Street, 14th May 1945.

Final Thoughts

Gateshead has a much more interesting history than many people are aware of. Although this book is a social history, and concentrates on the way in which people have lived – often through necessity rather than choice – over the last 150 years, many outside events have influenced this.

The Great Reform Act of 1832 was followed by the passing of the Municipal Corporations Act in 1835, which in turn led to the development of town councils. Under the Act, Gateshead received its first council in 1835. For much of the 19th century, the Council was made up of many of the industrialists and prominent businessmen of Gateshead – men who, by the nature of their industries, were already changing the face of the town. The development of these industries attracted waves of Scottish and Irish immigrants who flocked into Gateshead in ever increasing numbers putting a huge strain on the housing stock and basic sanitation provision. The administrative inexperience of the new council was shown by the findings of the Cholera Commissioners report of 1854 when Gateshead became the only Tyneside town to actually have a map drawn showing the location of cholera deaths in the third (and last) cholera epidemic in 1853. This highlighted the worst areas of town and, eventually, spurred the Council into at least some degree of activity.

Swinburne Street in the 1920s.

A huge swathe of Victorian reforms – factory acts, education acts, public health acts – were introduced during the latter part of the 19th century. Gateshead reacted to Forster's Education Act of 1870, in particular, with commendable speed with a major new school building programme throughout the town. The Factory Acts, which provided workers with statutory days off led to the rise of, and interest in, sports, while the Public Health Acts led indirectly to the formation of firstly, Windmill Hills Park, and later, Saltwell Park. Victorian legislation led to the creation of new parishes and consequently, many more churches and mission rooms in Gateshead, with Non-Conformist 'competitors' also creating more churches and chapels. Although many of these were abandoned, demolished or destroyed during the 20th century, they still had an effect on the landscape.

The Tramways Act of 1870 ultimately led to the introduction of steam trams, which were followed by electric trams – a form of transport which lasted till 1951 in Gateshead. This meant that as workers could now be more mobile, new housing could be developed in outlying areas such as Redheugh, the Teams, Bensham and Low Fell. Much of this housing was in the form of the 'Tyneside flat', a new concept credited to a Gateshead builder, William Affleck.

Development, innovation and change are continuous processes. This means that many of the new buildings of the Victorian era (and a number of the 20th century buildings too!) are no longer with us, which gives us the opportunity to ask the question 'Do you remember … ?'

I hope this book brings back many of these memories and prompts you to remember others. I have enjoyed writing it; I hope you enjoy reading it.

These were the images that were thought appropriate for a 1950s postcard of Gateshead.

Summerhill Books

Summerhill Books publishes local history books on Newcastle, Gateshead, North Tyneside Northumberland and Durham.

To receive a catalogue of our titles send a stamped addressed envelope to:

Andrew Clark, Summerhill Books, PO Box 1210, Newcastle upon Tyne NE99 4AH

or email: summerhillbooks@yahoo.co.uk

or visit our website to view our full range of books:

www.summerhillbooks.co.uk

Also available

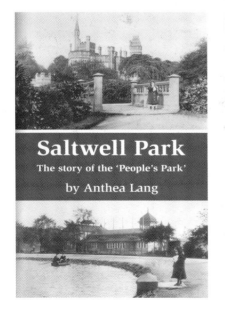

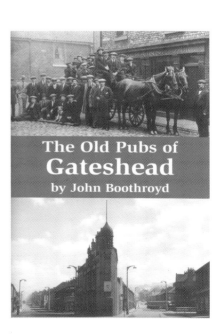